GUIDE TO THE ANTIQUITIES OF
ROMAN
BRITAIN

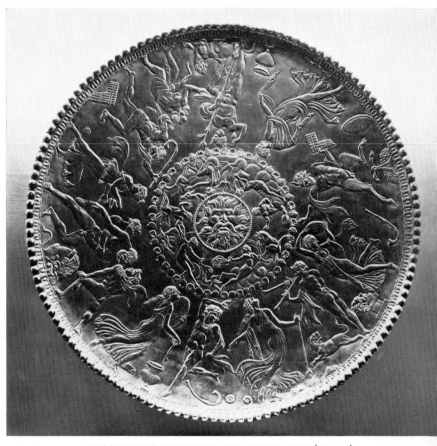

MILDENHALL TREASURE: THE GREAT DISH (II, *c.* 9)
Diam. 1 ft. 11¾ in.   p. 40

GUIDE TO THE ANTIQUITIES OF

ROMAN

BRITAIN

PUBLISHED BY

THE TRUSTEES OF THE BRITISH MUSEUM

LONDON

SBN 7141 1307 7

First published 1951
Second edition 1958
Third edition 1964
Reprinted 1966
Second reprint 1971

The illustration on the cover shows the bronze parade
helmet from Ribchester, Lancs., (p. 67, and plate xxvi, 4).

MADE AND PRINTED BY OFFSET IN GREAT BRITAIN BY
WILLIAM CLOWES AND SONS, LIMITED, LONDON, BECCLES AND COLCHESTER

PREFACE TO THE THIRD EDITION

THE purpose of this Guide, which was first issued under my predecessor, Mr. A. B. Tonnochy, is to offer a survey of the antiquities of Roman Britain illustrated by representative pieces from the British Museum's collection. These include all the exhibits that are of outstanding interest, whether in their own right or because of their archaeological associations.

The scheme of the Guide is a short general introduction on Roman Britain, followed by a series of sections illustrating the various aspects of its life and art, with detailed references to select pieces.

For assistance in the preparation of the first edition the Trustees are indebted to Professor I. A. Richmond, who read through the text and made valuable comments and suggestions; Dr. D. B. Harden, who revised the section dealing with glass vessels; Mr. R. P. Wright and Mr. M. H. Callender, for a note on the inscription on an amphora neck from the Walbrook, and to various persons and institutions who have given permission for the use of illustrations, whose names are given in their places.

The Guide is the work of Mr. J. W. Brailsford, M.A., F.S.A., F.M.A., Deputy Keeper in charge of the Sub-Department of Prehistory and Roman Britain.

R. L. S. BRUCE-MITFORD
*Keeper of British and
Medieval Antiquities.*

CONTENTS

PART ONE: ROMAN BRITAIN

PART TWO: ANTIQUITIES OF ROMAN BRITAIN

FIG. 1. Map of Roman Britain
(*After I. A. Richmond in 'Roman Britain' ('Britain in Pictures'), by courtesy of I. A. Richmond and Messrs. Adprint Ltd.*)

PART ONE

ROMAN BRITAIN

1. *The Background*

AT the time of the Roman Conquest, the inhabitants of Britain were
divided into a number of peoples, diverse in culture and constantly
warring with each other. They were by no means all the woad-painted
savages of popular imagination. In the south the war-like Belgae were
established, latest arrived of the prehistoric peoples of Britain, who had
come over to Kent from the Continent rather over a century before,
and were still expanding westwards. The Belgae were familiar with
many of the material elements of civilization; their kings minted and
circulated their own coinage and they imported wine and other Roman
luxuries from the Continent.

Outside the Belgic area were other tribes, such as the Brigantes of
Yorkshire, still in a condition of barbarism, and ultimately, in the in-
accessible highlands of the north and west, there lived the primitive
descendants of Bronze Age folk and poverty-stricken colonies of refugees
from Gaul.

Within this heterogeneous assemblage of peoples there was constant
warfare; the Belgae not only prosecuted continual wars of expansion
against the non-Belgic tribes, but those north of the Thames, the Catuvellauni, were at war with the Atrebates of Hampshire.

In spite of their warlike preoccupations, these Britons of the prehistoric Iron Age were able to develop a splendid curvilinear style of
decorative art. Even after their economic and political activities had
been largely moulded to the Roman pattern, this thoroughly un-Roman
artistic tradition was still sufficiently vigorous and deep-rooted to per-
sist throughout the Roman occupation, and even beyond.

2. *Historical Summary*

Ever since Caesar's expeditions of 55 and 54 B.C., Britain's wealth in
minerals and corn, as a source of recruits for the army, and in other ways,
had presented an attraction to the Romans which made its ultimate
annexation almost inevitable. There were political reasons for conquest
as well; Britain had become a harbour for refugees from Gaul, a breed-
ing-ground of disaffection, and a base for active raids against Roman
territory. The Emperor Claudius was anxious to establish himself by a

resounding military triumph. Britain should plainly be his objective, and his opportunity came with the death of Cunobelin, the great King of the Catuvellauni, and the subsequent disruption of his kingdom.

The moment was ripe for invasion, and in A.D. 43 Claudius landed a large force on the East Kent coast. This army numbered 40,000–50,000 men, and was made up of four legions (possibly with at least a part of a fifth), and auxiliary troops. The first stage of the advance was rapid. After a decisive victory on the Medway, the legions crossed the Thames in the presence of the Emperor himself, and soon after the Catuvellaunian capital of Colchester was taken. The conquest of Wessex followed, and by 47 the boundary of occupied territory had spread to the line of the Fosse Way, from Lincoln to Seaton in Devon. Progress was checked in 61 when the Iceni of East Anglia rose in rebellion under their queen, Boudicca. Colchester, St. Albans, and London were sacked, and the rebels were only defeated after heavy Roman losses. After this setback, the Roman advance continued; Wales and northern England were subjected, and in 84 Agricola defeated the Caledonians somewhere north of the Tay at the battle of Mons Graupius. This was the northern limit of Roman expansion and in 122 Hadrian consolidated a frontier from the Tyne to the Solway by ordering the construction of the great wall which now bears his name. Although the wall seems to have been an effective barrier, the tribes of southern Scotland continued to be troublesome. Under Antoninus Pius the frontier was again carried north, and in 142 the building of a second wall across the Forth–Clyde isthmus was put in hand. The new wall did not last for long. About 197 the governor, Clodius Albinus, withdrew most of the troops from Britain to support his bid for the Imperial throne. As a result, the barbarians broke through the northern defences, leaving a trail of destruction in their wake. The Antonine Wall was never again occupied, but between 197 and 208 Hadrian's Wall was restored by Severus, who followed up his restoration of the frontier with a punitive expedition into Scotland. The turbulent tribes north of the wall were henceforth kept under strict military control by means of outpost garrisons.

Britain now enjoyed a century of peace. Towards the end of the third century, however, a new danger developed, no longer by land from the barbarians of the north, but by sea from Saxon and Irish raiders. Civil war also once again took its toll. In 287 Carausius, commander of the British Fleet, usurped the sovereignty of Britain. Constantius recaptured the Province in 296, but the troops which Allectus, the murderer and successor of Carausius, opposed to him included the frontier garrisons, and once again the wall was sacked. Constantius not only restored Hadrian's Wall, but developed a system of coastal forts between the

Wash and the Solent (the 'Saxon Shore') as a precaution against sea-raiders.

Hitherto attacks on Britain had been uncoordinated, but at last in 367, a great combined force of Saxons and Irish, with Picts from the Scottish Highlands, descended simultaneously from the east, west, and north. The wall was overrun and the whole province devastated. The defeat of the barbarians by Count Theodosius in 369 brought a temporary return of peace, but hardly of prosperity; the wall was again restored, and the coastal defences were reinforced by a system of look-out towers built along the Yorkshire coast. In 383, however, a bid to

FIG. 2. Costume in Roman Britain
(*After M. and C. H. B. Quennell in 'Everyday Life in Roman Britain',
by courtesy of Messrs. B. T. Batsford, Ltd.*)

seize the throne was made by Magnus Maximus. Defence of the northern frontier was now left to *foederati*, allied troops drawn from the tribes of the frontier region, who since the time of Severus had become increasingly Romanized.

The end of the Province was drawing near. Soon after 400 Britain was again drained of troops by Constantine, who had been chosen Emperor by the troops in Britain from among their own ranks. In 410 Rome was sacked by the Goths; in the same year Honorius told the British communities that they must fend for themselves. A document called the 'Notitia Dignitatum', dated 428, indicates the presence of Roman troops in Britain at that time, but it may show a theoretical establishment rather than an actual state of affairs. It seems likely that the central government of the Province broke down, and that its effective union with the Empire ceased about the date of Honorius' decree.

3. *Dwellings*

The Britons were not urban-minded, and the towns which the Romans developed and founded became little more than markets and administrative centres. The simplest type of town-house was a long building at right-angles to the street, with its entrance at the end facing the street. The front part would serve as a shop or workshop, and might be completely open; the living-quarters were on an upper floor. The houses of officials and wealthy merchants were more elaborate, with rooms grouped along a main corridor or veranda, or the rooms might be ranged round a central rectangular courtyard.

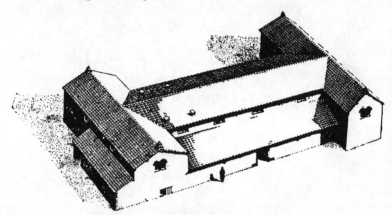

FIG. 3. Restoration of the Roman Villa at Park Street, Herts., during the late second century

(*After Dr. Norman Davey, in 'The Archaeological Journal', vol. cii.*)

The houses of owners of agricultural estates are known as 'villas'. Such houses were most commonly in the form of a long range of rooms with a projecting wing at each end, and a veranda or corridor along the face of the building between the wings. The entrance was in the centre of the veranda. Such a building might form one side of a quadrangular enclosed yard, often with slaves' quarters and farm buildings ranged round the other sides. Like the larger town-houses, villas were well-appointed, and the principal rooms might be floored with elaborate mosaic pavements. Such rooms might be warmed by a 'hypocaust', a form of central heating in which hot gases from a furnace circulated under the floor and through ducts in the walls.

All the rural population did not live in villas. On the downs of Wessex and the highlands of the north and west, native peasants continued to live in settlements and farmsteads of prehistoric type. These consisted of irregular groups of primitive huts, or, perhaps in Wessex, large communal houses. The area in which the latter occur may have been a great Imperial estate, which was worked by the peasant occupiers. Even in such primitive settlements Roman influence is shown by the presence of coins and superior pottery, and even, at Woodcuts in Dorset, painted wall-plaster.

4. *Agriculture*

We have seen that farming was carried out both on privately owned villa-estates and also on Imperial domains worked by native peasants. Such Imperial estates existed not only in Wessex, where arable farming eventually gave place to sheep-raising, but also in the Fens, where an enormous work of drainage and agricultural development was carried out.

It was once thought that the heavy plough with a coulter, capable of turning a proper slice even in a clay soil, was introduced to Britain by the Anglo-Saxons, but we now know that it was not only used in Roman Britain, but had been introduced before the Roman conquest by the Belgae. It is also possible that the villa-system had a Belgic origin, since cases are known where a Belgic farm developed into a villa.

Corn was the principal crop grown in Roman Britain, and there is some evidence that the Romans developed market-gardening and fruit-growing, besides the culture of vines for wine.

5. *Industry and Trade*

The great development of centralized industries during the Roman occupation was associated with the improved facilities for transport and trade provided by the Roman system of communications. The most striking feature of this system is the network of first-class roads, which can still be traced over long distances and frequently underlie modern highways. These roads were constructed primarily for military and administrative purposes, but were also available for the transport of merchandise. Ports were developed to deal with import and export trade, and inland barge-traffic passed along the Fenland drainage canals.

Commerce was also facilitated by the ubiquity of the Latin language, and the adoption of a uniform system of coinage, weights and measures.

The mineral wealth of Britain had been one of the chief incentives to annexation. The lead of the Mendips was being mined within a few years of the conquest; lead was also mined near Matlock, and elsewhere. Silver was extracted from the lead. Iron was mined in many localities; the ores in the Weald and the Forest of Dean were being worked on a large scale before the end of the first century. Cornish tin may have been mined during the first two centuries, and the industry was revived in the third century. Copper was mined on Anglesey, and gold at Dolaucothy in Carmarthenshire. Besides metals, coal was mined and widely used as fuel.

Wool obtained from sheep on the Imperial pastures in Wessex was woven into textiles at a government establishment at Winchester.

The manufacture of pottery, which in earlier days had been a domestic craft, became under the Roman occupation a highly specialized and centralized industry. Potteries developed in the New Forest, at Castor (Northants.), Crambeck (Yorks.), and elsewhere. Each produced distinctive wares which were traded over long distances (see Part Two, II, b).

The remains of industrial establishments are sometimes found in villas; for instance, fulling was probably carried out at the villas at Darenth in Kent and Titsey in Surrey.

6. *Art*

Romano-British art is best considered in immediate conjunction with illustrations of examples, which may be found in Part Two. The persistence of the native curvilinear decorative tradition is well shown on certain brooches (I, *d*), and Celtic skill in enamelwork survives on these and also on such objects as IV, *c*, 1–3. The native plastic art was stylized and abstract, and this tradition, too, survived in spite of an inundation of religious images and other works in the classical naturalistic style (IV, *a*, *b*, and see also II, *b*, 'Castor Ware'). The art of mural painting was commonly practised on the Continent, but has seldom survived in Britain, though there are many fine mosaic pavements from the Province (V, *b*), with designs perhaps imitating sumptuous but perishable carpets. Not only do some of the traditions of Romano-British art derive from prehistoric Britain, but elements of it outlive the Roman occupation. Thus the curvilinear 'trumpet-style' of I, *f*, 5 persists in the enamelled escutcheons of Dark Age 'hanging-bowls' and the illuminations of the seventh-century Book of Durrow.

7. *Religion*

Druidism, the national religion of the native Britons, with its organized hostility to Rome, was destroyed with the advance of the conquest, but the only positive religious demand made by the Romans was the observance of the official religion centred on Jupiter and the deified Emperor. The worship of local native deities was permitted and survived throughout the occupation. Such deities were sometimes identified with the classical gods whose worship was introduced by the Romans. The cosmopolitan nature of the Roman troops in Britain is reflected in the appearance of such exotic eastern cults as that of Mithras, and in the popularity of the Gallic Mother Goddesses.

Christianity was established in Britain in the second century. Under Constantine the Great it became in 312 the official religion of the Empire, and its acceptance in all levels of society in Britain during the fourth century is attested by historical accounts, and also by archaeological evidence such as the church at Silchester and the appearance of the sacred Chi-Rho monogram on villa floors, and on pewter- and silver-ware.

Temples of the standard classical type, with a pediment supported on columns and the whole building raised on a *podium*, are not common in Britain, the best examples being at Colchester and Bath. The circular or polygonal variety with external portico is also rare. The most typical Romano-British form of religious building was the 'Romano-Celtic' temple, which consisted of a small square building surrounded by a veranda.

8. *The Army and Military Works*

The backbone of the Imperial army was made up of the legions, which were always composed exclusively of Roman citizens. Each legion consisted of some 5,000 to 6,000 men, mostly heavy-armed infantry, but including a small detachment of cavalry. Amongst the legionaries were trained masons, carpenters, and engineers and other skilled artisans required for military construction work. A legion was commanded by a *Legatus legionis*, and divided into 60 'centuries', each under a centurion.

Auxiliary troops were raised in the provinces, and were grouped in cavalry *alae* or infantry cohorts, each with a strength of 1,000 (milliary) or 500 (quingenary). They were relatively lightly armed. The auxiliaries were expected to bear the main brunt of battle and frontier defence, while the citizen-legionaries were held in reserve.

Roman military encampments and permanent establishments were laid out according to a standard rectangular plan, which might be modified to suit the ground if need be. Even a temporary halting-place was defended by a ditch outside an earth rampart supporting a palisade; such temporary works are known as 'camps'. 'Forts' had a similar lay-out, but were designed as a permanent station for a cohort or *ala*. Their defences were more substantial than those of camps, and they contained permanent buildings such as long barrack-blocks, officers' quarters, headquarters buildings, granaries, workshops, and a hospital. Forts were built on the frontier or in military areas, but the enlarged version known as a 'fortress', and designed to contain a legion, is found in strategic positions in the rear of the frontier zones. Legionary fortresses were built in Britain at York, Chester, and Caerleon. The forts of the 'Saxon Shore' show the development of the theory of fortification by their thick, high walls and bastions for artillery.

Timber or stone towers within a palisade or wall (Signal Stations), such as were built along the Yorkshire coast in the fourth century, were used as look-out posts, from which warning could be given by a smoke or fire signal of the approach of hostile troops or ships.

The most impressive monument to the Roman occupation of Britain is the great frontier wall built by Hadrian. This was a massive stone wall some 15 feet high to the rampart-walk, with a six-foot parapet, and a great ditch in front; even in decay it is still imposing. It stretches from Wallsend, on the Tyne, to Bowness-on-Solway, a distance of 73 miles. The western part was at first built of turf, which was later replaced by stone. Forts were built at intervals along the wall, and at every mile was a fortlet, or 'mile-castle'. In each space between the mile-castles were two signal-turrets. Hadrian's Wall was not merely a static barrier to raiders; its forts and mile-castles were provided with gates opening to the north, through which the garrisons could sally out and 'roll up the enemy against the obstacle which he was attempting to cross' (I. A. Richmond, *Roman Britain* (1947), p. 16).

The inner boundary of the Wall zone was formed by the Vallum, a flat-bottomed ditch 20 feet wide by 10 feet deep with a bank on each side, which runs south of, and roughly parallel to, the Wall.

The Antonine Wall was a less elaborate structure than that of Hadrian, and shows a somewhat different tactical conception. It was built of turf, with nineteen forts closely ranged along its length, but no mile-castles or turrets.

9. *Government*

Imperial authority in the Province was exercised by a Legate, who was Governor and Commander-in-Chief, and by a Procurator, the head of the financial service. A considerable degree of self-government was allowed. The old tribal units became cantons, with councils responsible for the ordering of local affairs; urban communities were treated in a similar manner. Tribal representatives were sent to a central Provincial Council. In the early years of the occupation the tribal capitals were made centres for officially fostered Romanization.

The disastrous bid for Imperial power by Clodius Albinus led to the Province being divided into two as a precaution against governors becoming excessively powerful. In the reforms initiated by Diocletian at the end of the third century, it was again divided, this time into four.

10. *Survival*

The breakdown of the central provincial government and the withdrawal of Roman troops at the beginning of the fifth century meant the destruction of the material foundations of Roman culture in Britain.

AIR-PHOTOGRAPH OF THE ROMAN FORT AT HOUSESTEADS, NORTHUMBERLAND
Air Ministry, Crown Copyright Reserved. Ph. J. K. St. Joseph

Roads were no longer maintained, communications broke down, industry and trade collapsed. The closely knit Province disintegrated into a scatter of self-contained communities, and the Roman order became nothing but a splendid memory.

The gates were open to the barbarians who had been kept at bay for so long, and they were not slow to take advantage. There was, however, no concerted mass invasion, no sweeping military conquest and imposition of a new order. The Anglo-Saxons who were to settle and dominate the lowlands of Britain came, not in the great army of a highly integrated state, but in small and independent groups. There was no Anglo-Saxon *Blitzkrieg*, only a slow and insidious infiltration. Some came as *foederati*, mercenaries employed by the Britons as protection against the ravages of their more independent fellow barbarians. Others came prepared to win a foothold by the sword, but once established, they no doubt soon settled down and made contact with the Britons. In either case there must soon have been an intermingling of Romano-British and Anglo-Saxon blood and culture.

Even in the south and east, where the invaders soon became dominant, Romano-British culture survived sufficiently to assert itself in small things at least, and the beautiful enamelled escutcheons of the 'Hanging-Bowls' found in Anglo-Saxon graves may well have been made by the descendants of Romano-British craftsmen. Above all, Christianity, fostered in Roman Britain for over two centuries, was transplanted to the west by refugees, and there blossomed into the great and splendid growth of the Celtic Church.

PART TWO

ANTIQUITIES OF ROMAN BRITAIN

I. THE INDIVIDUAL

(a) Clothing

UNDER normal circumstances textiles soon decay, and it is only exceptionally that they are preserved from antiquity. There is no complete Romano-British garment in the collection, and only one considerable fragment of cloth from this period (1).[1] Types of Romano-British costume are shown in Fig. 2. Leather is more commonly preserved, and numerous shoes and other articles of apparel made from this material are included. Many are ornamented with elaborate openwork (3 and 4).

1. Cloth fragment, wool yarn, herring-bone stripe pattern, from late fourth-century signal station.　Huntcliff, nr. Saltburn, Yorks.　1912.6—30.1 1933.4—3.1

2. Shoes, leather, with other fragments.　Walbrook, London.　1935.11—6.6–50

3. Shoes, leather, from burial. (Fig. 4.)　Southfleet, Kent.　36.2—13.19, 20

4. Shoe, leather. (Fig. 4.)　London.　56.7—1.1006

5. Shoe, leather, with fresh hobnails. (Fig. 4.)　London.　56.7—1.1008

(b) The Toilet
(Fig. 5)

The Roman toilet was elaborate, and equipment for it was correspondingly varied, as may be seen from the examples illustrated.

Ligulae (3–5) were used for extracting cosmetics from the narrow glass phials in which they were kept (II, d, 15, 16).

Mirrors (6–8) were surfaced with (or made entirely of) 'speculum metal', which is a copper-tin alloy with a high percentage of tin.

The Roman bath was a protracted affair, in which the bather passed through a series of increasingly hot rooms, and finished with a cold plunge, as in the modern Turkish bath. Every town of any size had its public baths, and a visit to these was as much for social as hygienic reasons. After his bath, the Roman was anointed with oil, and then scraped with a strigil (11, 12).

[1] A piece of Roman cloth from the Walbrook was acquired in 1956 (1956, 12—1. 2).

1. Ear-scoop, bronze.	London.	56.7—1.1236
2. Ear-scoop with tweezers, bronze.	London.	56.7—1.1237
3. Ligula, bronze.	London.	56.7—1.1158
4. Ligula, bronze.	London.	56.7—1.1230

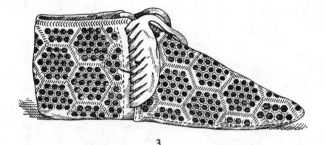

3

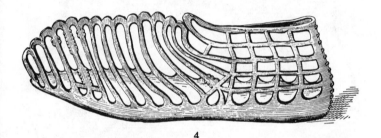

4

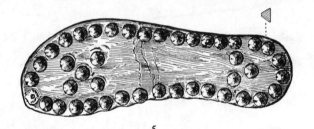

5

FIG. 4. Clothing (shoes) (I, *a*). ⅓. p. 10

5. Ligula, bronze.	?	1915.12—8.130
6. Mirror, speculum.	?	1907.10—24.3
7. Mirror, bronze with cover, repoussé medallions on top and bottom, that on cover containing a head of Nero.	Coddenham, Suffolk.	38.3—31
8. Mirrors, a pair of bronze (1924.12—13.43 illustrated).	London.	1924.12—13.42,43

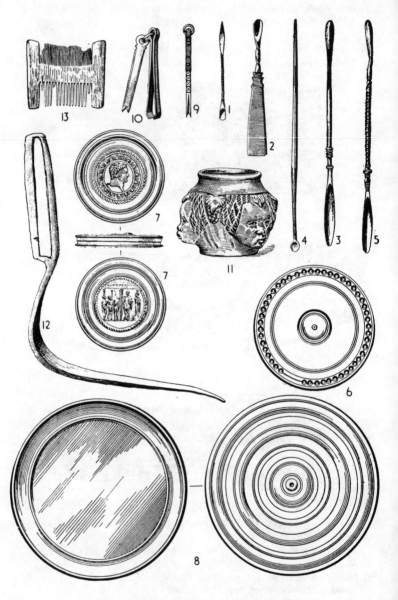

FIG. 5. Toilet articles (I, *b*). $\frac{2}{5}$. pp. 10–13

9. Nail-cleaner, bronze.	Wood Eaton, Oxon.	80.12—14.15
10. Nail-cleaner, with tweezers, bronze.	London.	56.7—1.1241
11. Oil-flask, bronze, with negroes' heads in relief, from a grave.	Bayford, Kent.	83.12—13.300

2 & 3 $\frac{1}{1}$

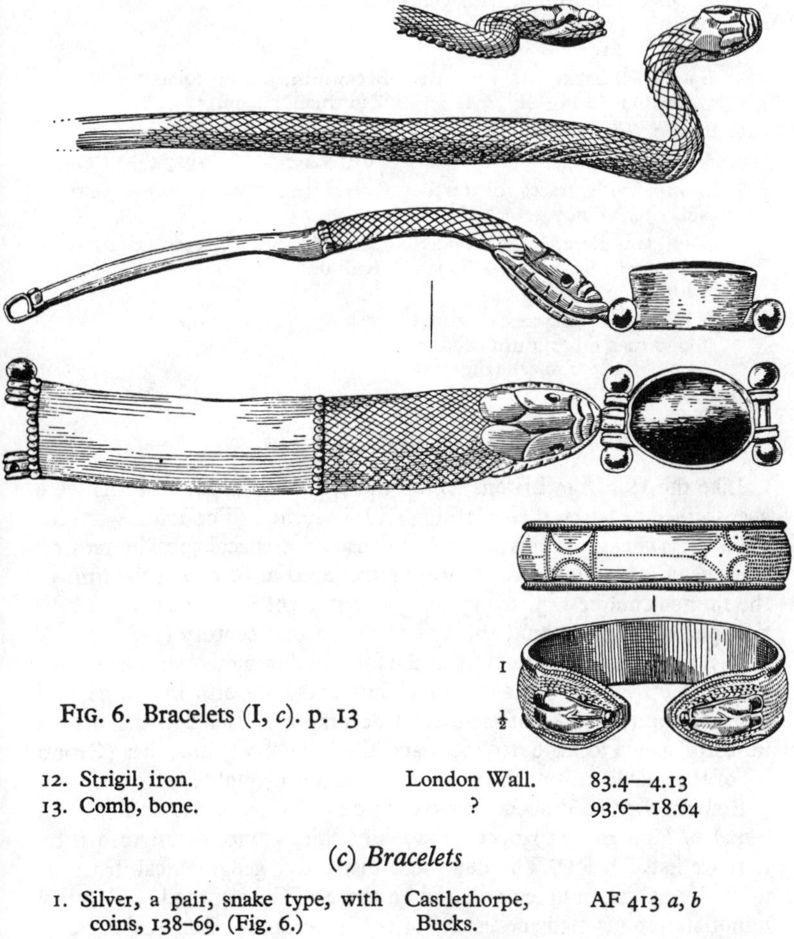

FIG. 6. Bracelets (I, c). p. 13 $\frac{1}{2}$

| 12. Strigil, iron. | London Wall. | 83.4—4.13 |
| 13. Comb, bone. | ? | 93.6—18.64 |

(c) Bracelets

1. Silver, a pair, snake type, with coins, 138–69. (Fig. 6.)	Castlethorpe, Bucks.	AF 413 a, b
2. Gold, snake type. (Fig. 6.)	Dolaucothy, Llandovery, Carmarthen.	Payne Knight Colln. 1824
3. Gold, snake type. (Fig. 6.)	Dolaucothy, Llandovery, Carmarthen.	Payne Knight Colln. 1824

The collection also includes two gold, two silver, and four bronze snake bracelets, from Bucks., Kent, London, and Norfolk. The two silver bracelets (83.12–13.554–9) were found at Slay Hill Saltings, Kent, with coins of Marcus Aurelius.

4. Gold, twisted wire. (Fig. 7.) Cf. 84.5—6.1, 2, from New Grange, Co. Meath, with gold rings and chain and denarius of Geta (d. 212).	Sussex.	Payne Knight Colln. 1824
5. Gold, from Backworth Treasure, with coins to 139. (Fig. 7.)	Backworth, Northumberland.	50.6—1.5
6. Bronze. (Fig. 7.)	Cirencester.	1929.7—15.7
7. Bronze. (Fig. 7.)	Cirencester.	1929.7—15.10
8. Bronze, with traces of textile adhering. (Fig. 7.)	Cirencester.	1929.7—15.11
9. Gold, two-piece, with applied gold-wire ornament. Found with I, f, 6. (Pl. 3.)	Rhayader, Radnor.	1900.11—22.1
10. Gold, hollow, wiry ends twisted round each other, third century (one of three similar). (Fig. 7.)	York.	1941.5—6.1

(d) Brooches

Like the Iron Age Britons whom they conquered, the Romans were accustomed to fasten their clothing with brooches. (The Latin word for a brooch is *fibula*, and this is commonly used in archaeological literature.) Various novel types of brooch were introduced to Britain at the time of the Roman conquest (3, 10, 13, 26, 33), but in the main the native tradition persisted until about the end of the second century (4–8, 14, 15), and is manifested most notably in the form and ornament of the 'Trumpet' (Group R) and 'Dragonesque' brooches, but also in the general and accomplished use of enamelled decoration. After 200 the British industry seems to have declined, and the 'Crossbow' brooches (Group T) of the third and fourth centuries are a continental type.

Romano-British brooches have been classified by R. G. Collingwood (*Arch. of Rom. Brit.*, 1930, chap. xv). The chief groups distinguished by him are listed below. The dates and distinctive geographical distributions (if any) given here are based on those of Collingwood, with a few minor alterations made necessary by recent research[1]. Each major group is illustrated by one or more examples selected from the collection.[2]

[1] See also C. F. C. Hawkes and M. R. Hull, *Camulodunum*, pp. 308 ff., especially Types III and IV.

[2] In the drawings of brooches decorated with coloured enamel, the colours are indicated according to the heraldic conventions, i.e. vertical shading, red; horizontal shading, blue; oblique shading, green; stippling, yellow.

FIG. 7. Bracelets (I, *c*). ⅔. p. 14

GROUP A. *One-piece, early.* Pre-conquest, first century.

    1. Bronze. (Fig. 8.)   Piecombe Hill, Sussex.   1920.11—9.6

    2. Bronze. (Fig. 8.)   Hod Hill, Dorset.   92.9—1.715

GROUP C. *'Aucissa.'* Called after the maker's name, which sometimes appears on the head of the brooch. A Gallic type. First half of first century.

    3. Bronze. (Fig. 8.)   London?   81.9—9.22

GROUP E. *Catch-plate pierced with key-patterns.* Normally first century.

    4. Bronze. (Fig. 8.)   ?   68.7—9.61

GROUP F. *Catch-plate pierced with several round holes.* First century.

    5. Bronze. (Fig. 8.)   Mildenhall, Suffolk.   W.G. 2340

GROUP G. *Plain rod-bow.* First and second centuries.

    6. Bronze. (Fig. 8.)   Littleton Farm, Dorset. 92.9—1.1592

It seems desirable to differentiate a further group of the same general, native-derived form as E–H, but without the distinctive features of E, F, or H, and differing from G in that the bow expands towards the head in somewhat the manner of the 'Trumpet' brooches. This group may be called G i.

    7. Bronze. (Fig. 8.)   Tuddenham, nr.   1928.12—5.1
                             Mildenhall, Suffolk.

GROUP H. *'Dolphin.'* First century and first half of second century, in southern Britain.

    8. Bronze. (Fig. 8.)   ?   1915.12—8.101

GROUP K. *Segmental strip bow.* Pre-Flavian.[1]

    9. Bronze. (Fig. 8.)   Colchester.   56.6—27.61

There is one variant of Collingwood's Group K which should be picked out and distinguished as a separate Group. This is the type which Wheeler has named, after the example shown below, the *'Langton Down'* brooch (*Lydney Report*, p. 71). We may here call such brooches Group K i. They are a Gaulish type, introduced to southern England by pre-Conquest trade, and by the Conquest. Pre-Conquest and pre-Flavian.

    10. Bronze. (Fig. 8.)   Langton Down,   92.9—1.1596
                           Dorset.

GROUP L. *Strip bow, half decorated, half plain.* Pre-75. Foreign type.

    11. Bronze. (Fig. 8.)   Colchester.   70.4—2.38

    [1] The 'Flavian' period extends from the accession of Vespasian in 69 to the death of Domitian in 96.

Fig. 8. Brooches (I, *d*). $\frac{2}{3}$. pp. 16, 18

GROUP N. *Tapering bow.* Middle and late second century. Found in Lower Severn Valley, and eastward to Oxon. and Berks. Ultimately derived from L.

12. Bronze. (Fig. 8.)   Town Malling, Kent.   78.11—1.265

GROUP P. *Winged bow, or 'Hod Hill'.* Claudian. Foreign type.

13. Bronze, traces of tinning. Hod Hill, Dorset.   92.9—1.748
    (Fig. 9.)

GROUP Q. *Head-stud.* Second century.

14. Bronze, red and blue enamel. Faversham, Kent.   1078—70
    (Fig. 9.)
15. Bronze, red and other enamel, Kingsholm, Glos.   70.10—13.24
    (Fig. 9.)

GROUP R. *Trumpet.* Fullest development in the north during first half of second century.

16. (R i) Bronze. (Fig. 9.)   ?   78.11—1.269
17. (R ii) Silver-gilt, a pair, from Backworth,   50.6—1.15, 16
    the Backworth Treasure, Northumberland.
    with coins to 139. (Fig. 9.)
18. (R ii) Silver, a pair, dated to Chorley, Lancs.   50.11—6.2, 3
    c. 140 by coins. (Fig. 9.)
19. (R iii) Bronze, three settings Stowting, Kent.   1904.6—28.2
    for enamel? at head. (Fig. 9.)
20. (R iv) Bronze, design on head Nr. Mildenhall,   1935.3—5.2
    originally inlaid with red Suffolk.
    enamel. (Fig. 9.)
21. (R iv) Bronze, traces of enamel Northchurch, Herts.   93.4—9.4
    including red, on upper bow.
    (Fig. 10.)

GROUP S. *Other Trumpet-headed.* First (S iii, Colchester) and second centuries.

22. (S i, Fantail.) Bronze, niello Brough Cas.,   57.12—14.25
    inlay. (Fig. 11.) Westmorland.
23. (S ii, Plate on bow.) Bronze, Probably Lincoln.   66.12—3.142
    front tinned or silvered,
    originally enamelled. (Fig.
    11.)
24. (S ii) Bronze. (Fig. 11.) Probably Lincoln.   66.12—3.141
25. (S iii, Fantail and plate.) Colchester.   70.4—2.51
    Bronze, originally enamelled.
    (Fig. 11.)

GROUP T. *P-shaped.* Common on Continent first and second centuries, but rare in Britain until third century (early 'crossbows'). Developed 'crossbows' date from fourth century.

26. ('Eye' brooch.) Bronze. (Fig. Northumberland.   1921.1—3.1
    10.)

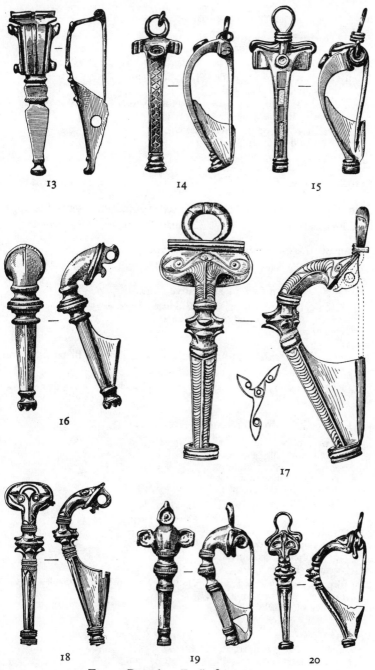

FIG. 9. Brooches (I, *d*). $\frac{2}{3}$. p. 18

27. ('Crossbow' brooch, early.) Colchester.   70.4—2.28
    Bronze, tinned or silvered.
    (Fig. 10.)
28. ('Crossbow' brooch, de- Odiham, Hants.   44.7—9
    veloped.) Gold. (Fig. 10.)
29. ('Crossbow' brooch de- Stowting, Kent.   1904.6—28.5
    veloped.) Bronze. (Fig. 10.)
30. ('Crossbow' brooch, late.) Colchester.   70.4—2.24
    Bronze gilt. (Fig. 10.)

GROUP U. *Divided bow*
31. Bronze. (Fig. 11.)   Nr. Chepstow, Mon.   91.3—27.21

GROUP V. *Knee*. Foreign type, introduced to Britain mid-second century.
32. Bronze. (Fig. 11.)   Brough, Westmorland.   1902.8—16.3

GROUP W. *Thistle*. Claudian. Foreign type.
33. Bronze. (Fig. 11.)   Hod Hill, Dorset.   92.9—1.720

GROUP X. *Bow and fantail*. Derivative of W.
34. Bronze, front tinned or sil- Wickham (Berks. or   78.11—1.266
    vered, originally inlaid with   Hants).
    red enamel. (Fig. 11.)

GROUP Y. *Bow-fronted*. Common on Continent, rare in Britain. Second
century.
35. Bronze, traces of enamel. Walbrook, London.   1934.12—10.14
    (Fig. 11.)

Disk brooches. Most common in second century.
36. Bronze, back tinned or sil- ?   O.A. 244
    vered, part gilt, glass boss;
    spaces between ribs decor-
    ated by stamp with diagonal
    cross in rectangle. (Fig. 11.)
37. Bronze, red and blue enamel. London.   52.3—22.1
    (Fig. 11.)
38. Bronze, red, yellow, white, ?   97.3—23.2
    and blue enamel, with figure
    of dolphin mounted in
    centre. (Fig. 12.)
39. Bronze, with applied plate Brough, Westmorland. 1902.8—16.5
    ornamented with repoussé
    design of triskele. (Fig. 11.)

Plate Brooches
40. Bronze, sitting hen, traces of Brough Cas.,   57.12—14.22
    red and other? enamel. (Fig.   Westmorland.
    11.)

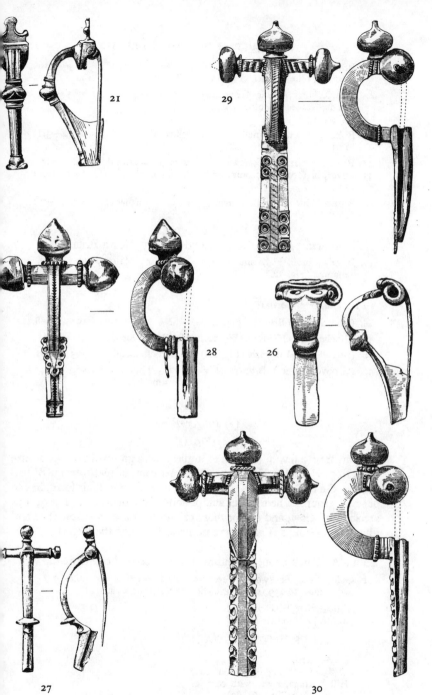

21

29

28 26

27 30

FIG. 10. Brooches (I, *d*). ⅔. pp. 18, 20

41. Bronze, man on horse, remains of   Nr. Woodyates,   92.9—1.1600
     red and blue enamel. (Fig. 11.)   Dorset.

42. Bronze, horse, settings for enamel   ?   72.5—20.8
     studs, traces of blue enamel.
     (Fig. 11.)

43. Bronze, rabbit, enamelled. (Fig.   Lincoln.   66.12—3.143
     11.)

44. Bronze, swastika. (Fig. 12.)   Brough, Westm'l'd.   74.12—28.4

45. Silver, in form of dolphin. (Fig.   London.   56.7—1.971
     12.)

46. Bronze, blue and yellow enamel.   Castor, Northants.   1909.6—7.1
     (Fig. 12.)

'Dragonesque' Brooch. Early second century. North Britain.

47. Bronze, blue, red, and yellow   Norton, nr. Malton,   62.7—1.18
     enamel. (Fig. 12.)   Yorks.

Penannular Brooches

48. (Coiled ends.) Bronze. (Fig. 12.)   ?   1915.12—8.112

49. (Pinched ends.) Bronze. (Fig. 12.)   Hod Hill, Dorset.   92.9—1.759

50. (Milled knob.) Bronze. (Fig. 12.)   Walbrook, London.   1934.12—10.6

51. (Grooved knob.) Bronze. (Fig.   Kirkby Thore,   57.12—14.12
     12.)   Westmorland.

(e) *Finger-Rings*
(Fig. 13)

Apart from a few quite plain examples, and a group of inferior bronze rings from Hod Hill, Dorset, about 80 per cent. of the Romano-British rings in the collection may be classified, according to their form, in one of seven groups. The features and periods of use of each of these groups are set out below, and one or more examples of each are described and illustrated. Groups A and B are numerically much the largest.

GROUP A. Thick hoop, expanding at bezel; second century.

1. Gold, from Backworth Treasure,   Backworth,   50.6—1.7
     with coins to 139; nicolo intaglio.   Northumberland.

     Also another, bezel with inscription
     to Mother Goddesses

     MATR/VM·CO·/COAE

     (50.6—1.10).
     Cf. 83.12—13.552, 553 from Slay
     Hill Saltings, Kent, with coins of
     Marcus Aurelius (161–80).

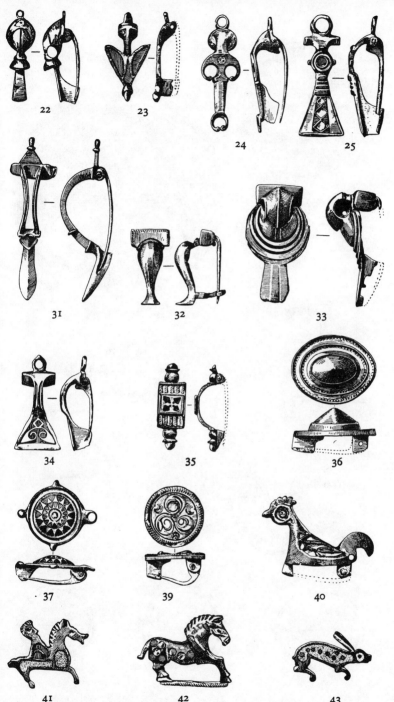

FIG. 11. Brooches (I, *d*). 22–5, 31–7, 39: $\frac{2}{3}$; 40–3: $\frac{4}{5}$. pp. 18, 20, 22

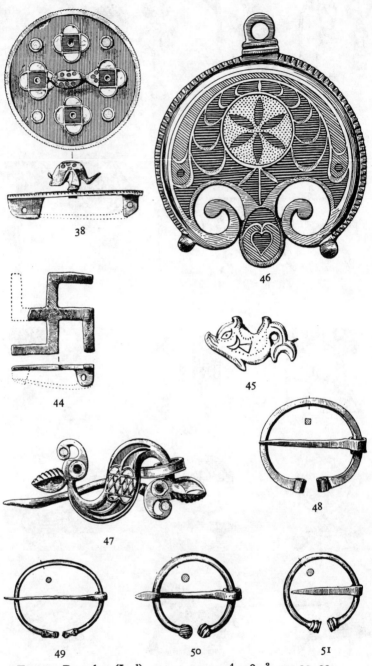

FIG. 12. Brooches (I, *d*). 44, 45, 47–51: $\frac{4}{5}$; 38: $\frac{2}{3}$, pp. 20, 22

FIG. 13. Finger-rings (I, *e*). ¼. pp. 22, 26

GROUP B. Bevelled shoulders, widening towards bezel; third and fourth centuries.

2. Gold; nicolo intaglio, Mercury. Sussex. AF 415
Cf. 1911. 10—26.1, 2 from Grovely
Woods, Wilts., with coins showing
date of deposition, c. 395; 1900.11
—23.1, 2, 3 from Sully Moors,
Cardiff, with coins to 306; AF 414
from Ilchester, Somerset, with
coin of Severus Alexander (222–
235) inset.

GROUP C. 'Humped' shoulders; third and fourth centuries. One (92.9—1.893) comes from Hod Hill, Dorset; most of the material from this site is Claudian.

3. Silver; nicolo paste intaglio, Mer-   Nr. Wittering,   1906.2—10
cury.   Northants.

GROUP D. Serpent rings.

4. Gold, from Backworth Treasure.   Backworth,   50.6—1.6
                                    Northumberland.

GROUP E. With pair of globules at each junction of hoop and bezel.

5. Gold, nicolo intaglio, ears of corn?;   Backworth,   50.6—1.8
also another; from Backworth   Northumberland.
Treasure.

GROUP F. Ribbon-hoop and square bezel; late fourth and early fifth century.

6. Silver, three together, found with   Amesbury,
coins to early fifth century.   Wilts.
Bezel engraved with gryphon?   57.6—30.1
Bezel engraved with four helmeted   57.6—30.2
heads.
Bezel engraved with stag and bird.   57.6—30.3

GROUP G. Filigree hoop; fourth to fifth centuries.

7. Gold, clasped hands in relief on   Richborough,   1936.2—4.1
bezel.   Kent.

(f) Miscellaneous Personal Ornaments

Amongst the various objects of personal adornment listed below, the fragment of *cloisonné* work (2), and the bronze mount in the 'trumpet' style (5) are of particular interest. *Cloisonné* technique, in which cells are built up from thin strips of metal to contain enamel or semi-precious stones, was not normally practised in this country before the fifth century. Our first-century example is therefore quite exceptional. The 'trumpet' style of (5) is a good example of the survival of the Celtic artistic tradition in Roman Britain.

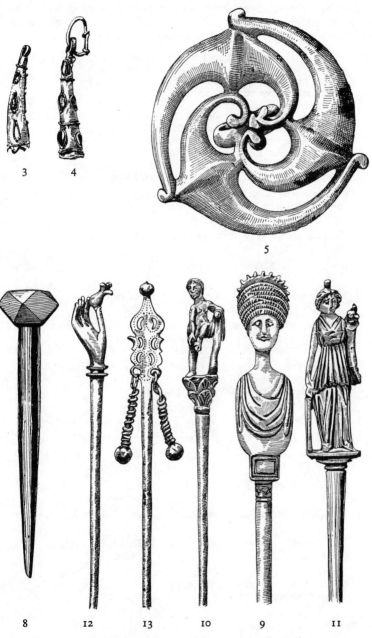

3   4

5

8   12   13   10   9   11

FIG. 14. Miscellaneous Personal Ornaments (I, f). $\frac{1}{1}$. p. 28

Relatively short and simple pins of bronze or bone were no doubt used, as an alternative to brooches, for securing garments. Elaborate examples such as (8–13) below were probably used as hairpins.

1. Chains, gold, a pair, each with figure-of-eight links, and with wheel and crescent pendants attached. From the Backworth Treasure; found with coins to 139. (Pl. 1.) — Backworth, Northumberland. — 50.6—1.3, 4

  Cf. gold chain, similar, with wheel pendants, found with snake bracelets. Llandovery, Carmarthen. (Payne Knight Colln. 1824.)

  Gold chain, similar, with denarius of Geta (d. 212), gold finger-rings, and bracelets. From New Grange, Co. Meath. (84.5—20.4.)

  Gold chain, similar, triple, from Hadrian's Wall near Newtown, Carlisle, with coins Nero–Marcus Aurelius. (1904.11—2.2.)

2. *Cloisonné* fragment, bronze and iron pyrites, with Belgic pottery and middle and late first century Samian. — Harpenden, Herts. — 1946.7—3.1

3. Ear-ring, gold, hollow. From a Roman villa. (Fig. 14.) — Ashtead, Surrey. — 1937.3—9.1

4. Ear-ring, gold, hollow. (Fig. 14.) — Walbrook, London. — 1934.12—10.2

5. Mount, bronze, triskele of peltas in 'trumpet' style. (Fig. 14.) — Icklingham, Suffolk. — 1935.4—16.1

6. Necklet?, rectangular gold plates set with carnelians or blue pastes, filigree borders. Found with 1, *c*, 9. (Pl. 3.) — Rhayader, Radnor. — 1900.11—22.2

7. Pendant, gold, 'ladder' form, set with blue-green stones and pearls; with bracelets, from burial of two children. (Pl. 1.) — Southfleet, Kent. — 1912.16—20.1

8. Pin, jet, faceted head. (Fig. 14.) — Lincoln. — 66.12—3.108

9. Pin, bone, female bust. (Fig. 14.) — ? — O.A. 245

10. Pin, silver, Venus with foot raised. (Fig. 14.) — City of London. — 83.5—9.3

11. Pin, bone, Fortuna. (Fig. 14.) — City of London. — 83.5—9.2

12. Pin, silver, hand holding pomegranate. (Fig. 14.) — Walbrook, London. — 1934.12—10.21

13. Pin, bronze, openwork head with pendants. (Fig. 14.) — Walbrook, London. — 1934.12—10.23

14. Plaque, gold, applied medallion with repoussé portrait of Faustina I, (d. 140). Filigree border. (Pl. 1.) — Colchester. — 70.4—2.23

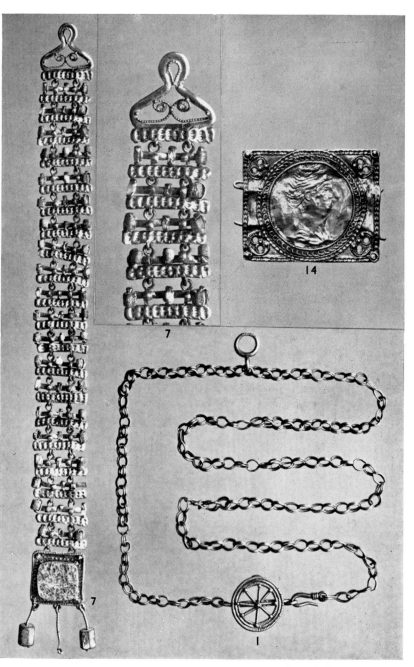

I. MISCELLANEOUS PERSONAL ORNAMENTS (I, f)
1:⅔ 7:⅔ (detail ¼) 14:¼ p. 28

II. SAMIAN POTTERY (II, 2). ⅓. pp. 28-30.

II. THE HOME: ARTICLES OF DOMESTIC USE

(a) Samian Pottery
(Pl. 2)

SAMIAN ware is the term generally used in this country to describe the red-glazed, mass-produced pottery which was used as 'best' tableware throughout the Roman Empire. It was carried even beyond the limits of the Empire by traders, and has been found as far afield as southern India. It has been classified by Dragendorff and others, and the periods when the different types were in use are known. Moreover, the potters frequently had their names stamped on the pots made in their factories, and even when such stamps are not present a decorated pot may sometimes be assigned to a certain potter by details of the ornament. Since the periods of activity of many Samian potters have been worked out, Samian ware is of great value in dating archaeological deposits in which it is found.

Nearly all the Samian ware used in Britain was imported, although a few small potteries are known to have existed in this country. (Cf. the 'waster' (82.8—29.2) from Aldgate, London.) During the late first century B.C. and the early first century A.D. the fine red-glazed pottery known as Arretine ware was made at Arretium (Arezzo) and elsewhere in Italy. It is of superior quality, both as regards fabric and ornament, but is very rare in Britain. Most first-century Samian ware in Britain came from La Graufesenque and other centres in South Gaul, whose products are distinguished by their glossy dark- or cherry-red finish. A pottery was founded at Lezoux, in central Gaul, c. 40, and during the second century the central Gaulish factories were the chief suppliers of the British market. They were active until c. 260. Their products are more orange in colour than the South Gaulish ware. Samian pottery was also made in East Gaul during the second century (at Trier until the middle of the third century), but relatively little of this pottery reached Britain.

Some of the commonest forms defined by Dragendorff are listed below, with examples taken from the collection.

Decorated

Form 29. Carinated bowl, with rouletting below rim, and beneath this two zones of decoration separated by a narrow plain moulding. First century.

1.   London.   1915.12—8.51

Form 37. Hemispherical bowl, with plain band below the rim, separated by an 'ovolo' from a zone of ornament. First made during Nero's reign, and predominates over 29 by c. A.D. 85.

| 2. | Uncertain, possibly Jordan Hill, Weymouth. | 79.7—12.28 |

Form 30. Cylindrical bowl. Early first to late second century.

| 3. | Sandy, near Bedford. | 44.9—28.2 |

Plain

Form 35 (small), *36 (large)*. Hemispherical cups with barbotine leaves on broad curved rim. 35—mainly Flavian. 36—Flavian and second century.

| 4. (35) | London. | 56.7—1.422 |
| 5. (36) | Wingham, Kent. | 94.3—9.18 |

Form 45. Mortarium (cf. II, *b*, 1). 'Wallside' type, with lion's-head spout. Late second-early third century.

| 6. | Billingsgate, London. | 1921.7—22.3 |

Form 18. Shallow platter, steep wall forming sharp angle with floor, bead-rim. First century.

| 7. From Roman villa. | Snodland, Kent. | 1948.4—2.3 |

Form 18/31. Wall more sloping than 18, floor depressed near edge, rising to central 'kick'. Domitian–Trajan.

Form 31. Floor still more curved, forming continuous line with wall, relatively deep. Hadrianic, and very common in second century.

| 8. | Near Arlesey, Beds. | 1915.12—8.78 |

Form 27. Bipartite cup. Late first century, lasts in diminishing numbers into second century.

| 9. | Suffolk Lane, London. | 53.5—2.35 |

Form 33. Conical cup. Claudian onwards; supersedes 27 in reign of Hadrian.

| 10. With burial in stone sarcophagus. | Harpenden, Herts. | 43.8—12.4 |

Form 72. Globular vase. Plain—first and into second century; with incised or barbotine ornament—to 200+.

| 11. | Felixstowe, Suffolk. | 81.6—26.9 |

Inkpot. All periods. These are common in Samian ware, but the specimen illustrated in Fig. 15 is made of a fine buff ware with brown coating.

12. With graffito IVCVNDI   Cannon Street,   1950.2—6
                      NDI   London.

The stamp illustrated (Pl. 3.) is one of the potter Cerialis, who was active at Lezoux during the reigns of Trajan and Hadrian.

Mention should be made of the large quantity of plain Lezoux ware

FIG. 15. Inkpot (II, *a*, 12). $\frac{1}{2}$. p. 31

in the collection from Pudding Pan Rock, Whitstable, Kent. This comes from the cargo of a merchant ship wrecked while sailing to Britain.

(1908.7—27; 1910.10—25; 1920.11—23; 1937.3—16; 1937.12—10; &c.)

A fine example of a Samian form occurring in black ware is the beaker with 'cut-glass' ornament from Reculver shown in Plate 3; it is probably of the late second or early third century. (1956.7—6.1.)

(b) Coarse Pottery

Romano-British coarse pottery was made in a wide variety of forms and fabrics, at numerous centres, each producing its own characteristic wares. Its study is therefore a detailed and complicated business, and it is difficult and perhaps positively misleading to attempt a general survey in a single section of a small Guide. Moreover, the significance of fabric is as great as that of form, and the characteristics of different fabrics can only be learnt by inspection and handling of actual pots.

All that the following account attempts is to set out some of the commonest forms and fabrics, with examples taken from the collection, together with a few pots of particular interest outside the categories detailed. The only concise survey of Romano-British coarse pottery hitherto published is that by R. G. Collingwood (*Arch. of Rom. Brit.*, 1930, chap. xiv). For want of a more up-to-date summary, the following account is based on this, but it has been modified in accordance with the most important recent publications.

GROUP A. *Mortaria*. (A mortarium is a large, strong bowl, usually with the inside roughened with grit, and used for pounding food.) Mortaria with bead-and-roll rims (such as that illustrated) were in use until *c*. 300. A rim of hammerhead section appears in the North during the late second century, and the 'wall-side' type of mortarium (similar to its Samian counterpart, II, *a*, 6) is another late type. There is an early type superficially somewhat resembling the 'wall-side' form, but it may be distinguished by its sloping 'wall' and thickened rim. The name or mark of the maker is frequently stamped on the rims of mortaria.

> 1. Mortarium, hard, sandy, buff ware; London.   56.7—1.44
>   with stamp]AṄDID[F]ECIT
>   retrograde. (Fig. 16.)

GROUP B. *Bowls*. These occur in many forms. That illustrated is an early type; other common forms are (*a*) bead-rimmed and other native-derived; (*b*) with broad, reeded rim, first and into second century; (*c*) flanged, c. 100+, becoming coarser in form.

> 2. 'Egg-shell' bowl, with scale orna- London.   81.9—9.16
>   ment; fine buff ware with brown
>   coating. (Fig. 16.)

GROUP C. *Dishes*. The periods of use of some principal types are as follows: (*a*) with flat rim projecting externally, second and third centuries; (*b*) with bead-rim, second to fourth century; (*c*) flanged, third and fourth centuries.

> 3. Flanged dish, dark, smooth-surfaced Colchester.   54.4—12.7
>   ware; a cross is scratched inside the
>   bottom. (Fig. 16.)

GROUP D. *Flagons*. These may be classified according to the form of the lip, as follows: (*a*) multiple-ring ('screw-neck'), first and second centuries, with increasing emphasis of the top ring; (*b*) double-ring, first and second centuries; (*c*) pinched lip, pre-Hadrian; (*d*) nipple-spouted, late third and early fourth century; (*e*) with top in the form of a human head, third and fourth centuries.

> 4. Flagon, early multiple-ring, hard Cannon St.,   54.11—30.23
>   cream ware. (Fig. 16.)   London.

GROUP E. *Jars*. From a wide variety of types the following may be selected: (*a*) with bead-rim, a native type, derivatives of which survive into the third century; (*b*) cordoned, another native type, degenerate forms of which last to the fourth century; (*c*) Ollae, at first with relatively narrow rim and often with acute-angled lattice ornament, then in the fourth century with rim wider than the body and obtuse-angled lattice;

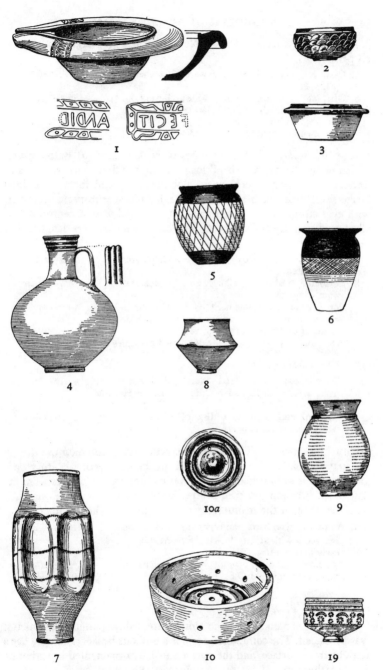

FIG. 16. Coarse Pottery (II, *b*). ⅙. pp. 32, 34, 35

(*d*) cooking pots, coarse and simple, all periods; (*e*) large storage jars, all periods.

5. Olla, early type, hard grey ware. (Fig. 16.) — Colchester. — O.A. 246

6. Olla, late type, brown sandy ware; originally smooth-surfaced; lattice round girth, upper part including top of rim painted black. (Fig. 16.) — Basing, Hants. — 76.2—5.1

GROUP F. *Beakers.* The chief types of beakers are: (*a*) Butt-beakers, which retain the native 'barrel' form during the first century, and later develop a tapering conical neck, globular body and foot; (*b*) Folded beakers; (*c*) Carinated beakers, chiefly, at least, first century; (*d*) globular, with everted lip, sometimes rough-cast, first and second centuries, but also fourth century at Crambeck; (*e*) 'Poppy-head' beakers, late first and second century.

7. Folded beaker, hard grey ware, dark-coated. (Fig. 16.) — Colchester. — 70.4—2.577

8. Carinated beaker, thin hard grey ware. (Fig. 16.) — Colchester. — 70.4—2.726

9. Poppy-head beaker, fine hard, dark, glossy-faced ware, with vertical bands of barbotine dots. (Fig. 16.) — Upchurch Marshes, Kent. — 1371—70

(See under 'Castor ware' for developed examples of butt-beakers.)

GROUP G. *Cheese-presses*

10. Cheese-press, sandy red ware; from a Romano-British building. (Fig. 16.) — Boxstead Farm, Lower Halstow, Kent. — 83.12—13.424

10 *a*. Ribbed and perforated disk of sandy grey ware. (Fig. 16.) — ? — 1925.11—19.1

GROUP H. *Amphorae.* The cylindrical type was in common use during the first and early second century. From the mid-second century on a globular form was normal, but this was common at Colchester from the date of the invasion and even before. Amphorae are sometimes stamped with the name of the manufacturer whose product they contain.

11. Amphora, cylindrical, sandy, brick-red ware, with stamp MAROF, early first century. (Fig. 17.) — Stanmore, Middx. — 1949.4—4.1

12. Amphora, globular, sandy, buff ware, with stamp J.Ɔ.Ƨ. (Fig. 17.) — Colchester. — 70.4—2.660

Castor Ware (Pl. 4)

This ware is named after the Northamptonshire potteries at which it was produced. The commonest form is a bulbous beaker; the ware has a dark lustrous surface, and the pots are usually ornamented in barbotine with spirited animal figures or foliate scrolls. This ornament retains

$\frac{3}{4}$

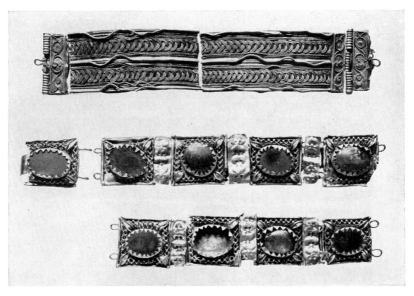

III

13

15

16

14

17

18

IV. COARSE POTTERY (II, *b*) ⅓ pp. 34, 35

much of the dynamic stylization of the native art tradition; compare it, for instance, with the mass-produced Roman Samian ware.

Castor ware was made from the late second century until the end of the Roman occupation.

13. Castor ware beaker, fine dark-coated ware, with chariot race in barbotine.	Colchester.	57.8—6.1
14. Castor ware beaker, fine dark-coated ware, with scroll ornament in white barbotine, and rouletting.	Castor, Northants.	1931.6—9.1
15. Castor ware beaker, fine white ware, dark-coated, with barbotine hunting scene.	?	75.6—5.5
16. Castor ware vase, fine dark-coated ware, with scroll ornament in white barbotine, and rouletting.	Duston, Northants.	1948.10—2.1

New Forest Wares (Pl. 4)

The New Forest potteries were active during the late third and fourth centuries. Before *c.* 300 they were turning out light wares with incised ornament; afterwards they produced pots of a characteristic hard ware, with a dark metallic surface, often with painted ornament, and also rosette-stamped bowls and other examples of the 'Fourth-century Red Ware' group (see below).

17. Bottle, fine hard ware with lustrous dark-brown surface and white-painted ornament.	New Forest.	58.3—18.4
18. Flask, fine hard red ware, with dark-brown coating and white-painted ornament.	New Forest.	58.3—18.1

Crambeck Ware

The most characteristic products of the kilns at Crambeck, in Yorkshire, are dishes, bowls, and mortaria of buff ware, ornamented in reddish-brown paint. The potteries were active throughout the fourth century, and particularly after *c.* 370.

Fourth-century Red Ware

A group of forms, late in date, mostly imitating Samian prototypes. The surface is usually red, but both ware and finish are vastly inferior to the originals. Bowls with stamped ornament of rosettes or other designs are characteristic.

19. Bowl, pale brown ware, with poor dull-red glaze and rosette-stamp ornament. (Fig. 16.)	Burnham, Bucks.	1914.2—9.1

Rusticated Ware

These pots were ornamented by applying wet clay to the surface, and dabbing it with the finger-tips. It was popular in the North from the later first century until Hadrian; the ornament was usually applied in irregular ridges. Other varieties occur in southern England.

Miscellaneous Pots

20. Amphora neck with painted inscription.[1] (Pl. 5.) — Walbrook, London. — 1935.11—6.5

21. Bowl, imitating Samian form 37. Native ware, fine, dark, fairly hard, smooth-surfaced. From an Iron Age/Romano-British cemetery. (Fig. 17.) — Jordan Hill, Weymouth. — 79.7—12.16

22. Cover, coarse grey ware, with incised ornament. Found with radiate? coin and part of a 'crossbow' brooch, c. 300. From New Forest pottery site. (Fig. 17.) — Linwood, Hants. — 1937.10—5.1

23. 'Face-urn', smooth buff ware. (Fig. 17.) — Colchester. — 70.4—2.526

24. 'Face-urn', hard buff ware with painted dedication to Mercury 'DO MIIRCVRIO'. (Pl. 5.) — Lincoln. — 66.12—3.47

25. Infant's feeding-bottle, fine buff ware. (Fig. 17.) — Colchester. — 70.4—2.558

26. Flagon, dull yellow-green lead glaze over fine buff ware. Late first or early second century. (Pl. 5.) — Colchester. — 54.4—12.6

27. Money-box, fine, hard, dark ware, smooth surface. (Fig. 17.) — Lincoln. — 97.9—13.1

28. Two toy pots, from floor of potter's hut. (Fig. 17.) — Islands Thorns Inclosure, New Forest. — 1925.12—17.2,3

29. Urn, with ring-handles, fine red ware, with band of rouletting round neck and brown-painted scroll and lattice; contained bronzes. (VI, c, 2.) (Pl. 5.) — Felmingham Hall, Norfolk. — 1925.6—10.32

Important Regional Collections

Colchester: Pollexfen Collection (70.4—2, 467 to 601, &c.).

Corfe Mullen, Dorset, from mid-first-century kiln: 1934.1—17; 1935.1—10; 1940.7—1.892 to 1000. Pottery, &c., from other sites in Bournemouth area is included in the Calkin Collection (1940.7—1).

[1] A recent interpretation of this inscription, by Mr. R. P. Wright and Mr. M. H. Callender, is as follows: [GEM]ELLVM | MVN(ATI) C(E)LER(IS) AVR(ELI) [V(ILICI)]; i.e. 'Twin wine: (produce) of Aurelius, [slave-bailiff] of Munatius Celer.'

20 $\frac{1}{5}$

24 $\frac{1}{4}$

26 $\frac{2}{5}$

29 $\frac{1}{6}$

V. COARSE POTTERY (II, b) p. 36

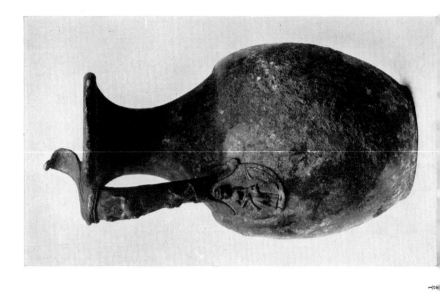

$2 \frac{1}{5}$

$3 \frac{1}{6}$

VI. METAL VESSELS (II, c)   p. 38

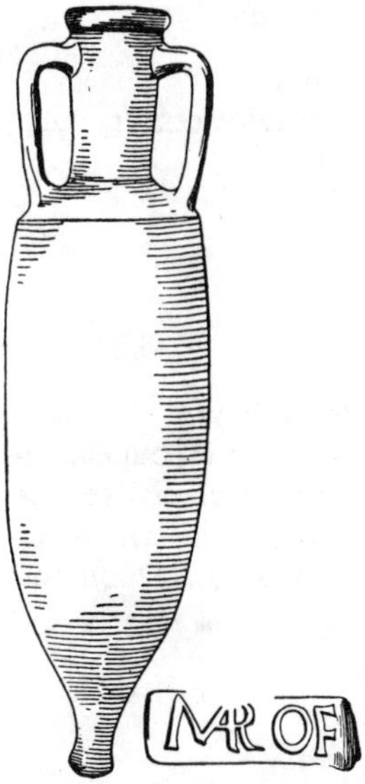

11 Ht. 3 ft. 6 in. Stamp $\frac{1}{3}$

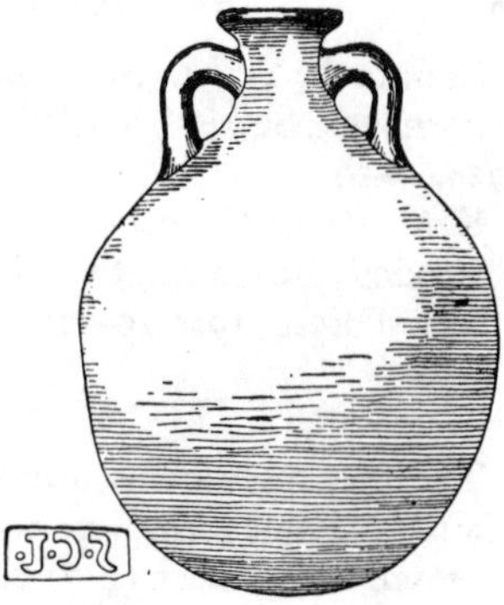

12 Ht. 2 ft. $3\frac{1}{2}$ in. Stamp $\frac{1}{3}$

21 $\frac{1}{6}$

22 $\frac{1}{9}$

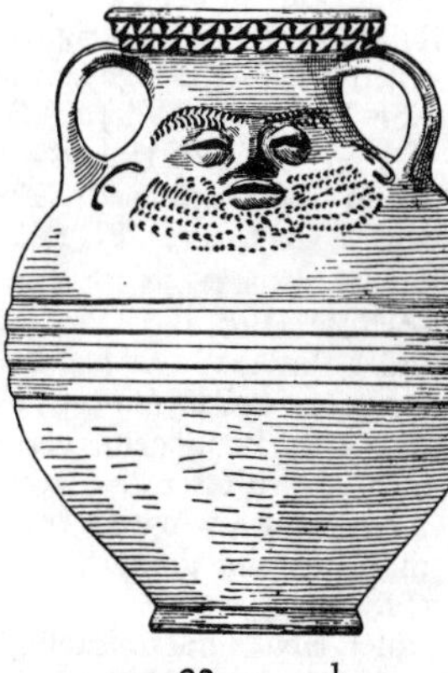

23 $\frac{1}{6}$

25 $\frac{1}{6}$

27 $\frac{1}{6}$

28 $\frac{1}{3}$

FIG. 17. Coarse Pottery (II, *b*). pp. 34, 36

Crambeck, Yorks., from kilns: 1932.12—8.18 to 53.
Farnham, Surrey (Snailslinch Farm), from late third-century kiln:
1926.6—19.
Kent: Payne Collection (83.12—13).
London: Roach Smith Collection (56.7—1).
New Forest: 1920.10—16; 1925.12—17.

(c) Metal Vessels

The first three items listed were probably for table use; skillets of relatively simple form were also used for domestic purposes, but elaborate examples such as (4–7) below might be used as sacrificial vessels. The skillet from Backworth (4) at least is of this type; the inscription on the handle is a dedication to the Mother Goddesses by Fabius Dubitatus.

1. Bowl, bronze, with maker's stamp 'AFRICANVS'. (Fig. 18.) — Luton, Chatham, Kent. — 94.8—3.58

2. Dish, silver, square with beaded edge and incised foliate ornament. (Pl. 6.) — Mileham, Norfolk. — 40.11—11.1

3. Jug, bronze; handle with figures of Diana, Actaeon, and hounds in relief, and bird's head terminals lying along lip. (Pl. 6.) — Faversham, Kent. — 1295—70

4. Skillet, silver, handle originally gilt, with relief floral designs and inscription MATR(IBVS) FAB(IVS) DVBIT(ATVS) inlaid with gold. From the Backworth Treasure, with coins to 139. (Pl. 18.) — Backworth, Northumberland. — 50.6—1.1

5. Skillet, bronze, with mask of Medusa. (Fig. 18.) — Faversham, Kent. — 82.4—5.1

6. Skillet, bronze: the handle is inscribed BODVOGENVS F (made by Boduogenus) and ornamented with scrolls executed in niello, and a winged genius, with monsters and dolphins in relief. (Pl. 18.) — Prickwillow, I. of Ely. — 93.6—18.14

7. Skillet, silver; the unintelligible inscription ΛΗ ΙΙΙΛ ΛΙΙ is inlaid on the handle: fourth or fifth century. (Fig. 18.) — ? (From a Welsh collection.) — 1942.1—7.1

8. Spoons, silver; group of five. (Fig. 18.) — Dorchester, Oxon. — 72.7—25.1–5

Cf. bone spoons with perforated bowls from Dowkerbottom Cave, Yorks., e.g. 57.11—13.29. (Fig. 18.)

Silver Treasures: The Mildenhall Treasure

The Mildenhall Treasure was acquired by the British Museum as Treasure Trove in 1946. It was reported that it had been accidentally

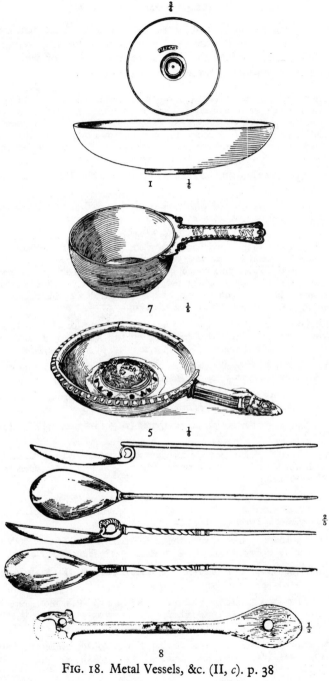

FIG. 18. Metal Vessels, &c. (II, *c*). p. 38

ploughed up during the War of 1939–45, on the edge of the Fens near Mildenhall in Suffolk. It consists of exceptionally fine and well-preserved fourth-century Roman silver ware, the owners of which no doubt buried it in order to preserve it from Saxon raiders.

9. Dish. 1 ft. 11¾ in. diam., 18¼ lb. weight. The outer frieze of relief figure-ornament shows in a lively fashion the triumph of Bacchus, God of Wine, over Hercules; Silenus and Pan are also shown, besides maenads and satyrs. There is an inner frieze of nereids riding on the backs of sea-monsters, and in the centre is a striking relief of Neptune or Oceanus. (Frontis.; 1946, 10—7.1; *Handbook*, No. 1.)

10, 11. Two platters with Bacchanalian figures in relief. (Pl. 7; 1946.10—7.2, 3; *Handbook*, Nos. 2, 3.)

12. Large dish, ornamented with close-meshed incised pattern inlaid with niello. (1946.10—7.4; *Handbook*, No. 4.)

13, 14. Bowl and lid. The flange of the bowl is ornamented with an incised foliate scroll originally inlaid with niello. The lid was probably not originally intended to go with the bowl; it is surmounted by the figure of a triton blowing on a conch, and is decorated with an upper zone of conventional foliate ornament and, beneath this, a relief frieze showing combats between centaurs and wild beasts, divided by human masks. (Pl. 7; 1946.10—7.11, 12; *Handbook*, Nos. 5, 6.)

15–18. Four large flanged bowls. The flanges are edged with large beads, and are ornamented with relief friezes of animals and trees, divided into sections by human masks. (Pl. 8; 1946.10—7. 5–8; *Handbook*, Nos. 7–10.)

19–20. Two small flanged bowls, the flanges ornamented with a form of vine-scroll (1946.10—7.9, 10; *Handbook*, Nos. 11, 12.)

21. A fluted bowl engraved with foliate ornament and a design of interlocked triangles. (1946.10—7.15; *Handbook*, No. 13.)

22, 23. Swing handles for 21, now detached (1946.10—7.16, 17; *Handbook*, Nos. 14, 15.)

24, 25. A pair of goblets, perhaps designed so that when inverted the base of each would serve as a small platter. (Pl. 8; 1946.10—7.13, 14; *Handbook*, Nos. 16, 17.)

26–30. Bowls, and 31–4, handles of ladles. The handles, which are now detached, are cast in the form of dolphins, and are partly gilt. (1946. 10—7.18–26; *Handbook*, Nos. 18–26.)

35. A 'christening' spoon, with the inscription PAPITTEDO VIVAS ('Long life to Papittedo'). (Pl. 8; 1946.10—7.28; *Handbook*, No. 27.)

36. A similar spoon with inscription to PASCENTIA. (Pl. 8; 1946.10—7.27; *Handbook*, No. 28.)

37–9. Three spoons, inscribed with the Christian Chi-Rho monogram between Alpha and Omega. (Pl. 8; 1946.10—7.29–31; *Handbook*, Nos. 29–31.)

40–2. Three spoons, the bowls decorated with foliate ornament. (1946. 10—7.32–4; *Handbook*, Nos. 32–4.)

10      $\frac{1}{4}$ II

13, 14 $\frac{2}{5}$

VII. METAL VESSELS (II, c) p. 40

17 $\frac{1}{5}$ 24 $\frac{2}{5}$

35 $\frac{1}{2}$

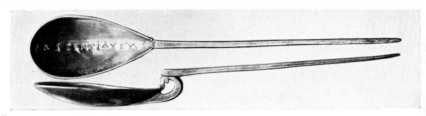

36 $\frac{1}{2}$

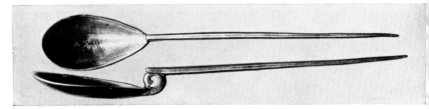

38 $\frac{1}{2}$

VIII. METAL VESSELS, ETC. (II, c) p. 40

44   ¾   43

47

45   ⅘   46

IX. METAL VESSELS, ETC. (II, *c*) p. 41

48   $\frac{4}{7}$

50   $\frac{1}{2}$

49   $\frac{1}{4}$

X. METAL VESSELS, ETC. (II, c)   p. 41

The Coleraine Treasure

We have here a sorry contrast to the splendidly preserved vessels in the Mildenhall Treasure. This was evidently a hoard of pirate's loot, and besides coins it consists only of ingots and the battered fragments of articles which have been broken up for greater ease in transport and sharing-out. The Coleraine Treasure was found at Ballinrees, near Coleraine, Co. Londonderry, in 1854, and the coins show that it was buried during the early fifth century. The most interesting pieces are listed below.

43, 44. Two ingots, stamped CVRMISSI and EX OF(FICINA)PA/TRICI ('from the factory of Patricius'). (Pl. 9; 55.8—15.1, 2.)

45, 46. Two pieces ornamented in 'chip-carving' style (a late-Roman technique which continued in use into the Migration Period). Both are ornamented with gilding and niello. 55.8—15.12, a corner of a rectangular article, with design of interlocking triangles. 55.8—15.13, a strip with scroll design; this is probably an ornamental band from a spear or staff. (Pl. 9.)

47. A handle, the end-plates with stamped ornament. (Pl. 9; 55.8—15.14.) Cf. fourth- to fifth-century continental work.

48. Hemispherical bowl with very thin walls, decorated with conventional plant and other impressed ornament. (Pl. 10; 55.8—15.31.)

The Coleraine Treasure also includes fragments of the heavily beaded rims of bowls or dishes (cf. the Mileham dish (2 above), and the Mildenhall Treasure), and a fragment of a dish with shallow-incised ornament as on the Mildenhall fluted bowl (21 above) and the Mileham dish.

The Capheaton Treasure

This small hoard consists of the handles of four skillets and a medallion, all with relief ornament portraying figures and scenes from classical mythology. It was found in 1747 at Capheaton, Kirkwhelpington, Northumberland, and was acquired with the Payne Knight Collection in 1824.

49. The finest handle is ornamented with a bust of Juno above Mercury in a niche, with Bacchus and Ariadne, a Naiad and a river-god below. (Pl. 10).

50. The medallion bears a relief showing Hercules and Antaeus wrestling. (Pl. 10.)

Pewter Ware: The Appleshaw Hoard

Silver table-ware was too expensive for any but the very wealthy. In the fourth century pewter (a tin-lead alloy) was extensively used as a cheap substitute; pewter ware was probably made in this country.

The Appleshaw Hoard takes its name from the place where it was

4

discovered, on the site of a Roman house near Andover, Hants. It consists
of ten large circular dishes with black inlaid pattern ornament (e.g. (53)
below), a dish (similar to (2) above), flanged bowls, a footed cup, a
flagon, a beaker similar in form to II, *b*, 7, small bowls, &c., besides the
two interesting pieces which are illustrated ((51) and (52) below).

51. Dish with incised fish; nearly pure tin. (Fig. 19; 97.12—18.32.)
52. Bowl inscribed with Chi-Rho monogram. (Fig. 19; 97.12—18.28.)
53. Dish with black inlaid pattern ornament. (Fig. 19; 97.12—18.10.)

The collection also includes many pewter vessels from Icklingham,
Suffolk, and other East Anglian sites. Three further specimens of
pewter ware are listed below.

54. Polygonal bowl. (Fig. 19.)	Icklingham, Suffolk.	53.4—11.2
55. Flagon. (Fig. 19.)	Church Norton, Sussex.	1926.4—12
56. Dish. (Fig. 19.)	Cirencester, Glos.	1929.12—9

(d) Glass Vessels

The Roman world learnt the use of glass from the ancient centres of
manufacture in Syria and Alexandria. By the time of the Roman invasion
of Britain glass ware was being made in Italy and southern Gaul, and
by about the end of the first century an industry was established in
Northern Gaul and the Rhineland, whence thereafter came much of the
glass used in Roman Britain. Even in Europe the glass workers were
often immigrant Syrians or Alexandrians. The windows of Roman
houses were often glazed and glass was also used for a variety of vessels,
some examples of which are listed below.

1. Amphora, pear-shaped, pale bluish-green; from a grave, contained cremated bones; late first or second century. (Pl. 12.)	Southfleet, Kent.	36.2—13.18
2. Beaker, colourless, with facet-cutting, late first or early second century, from a grave. (Pl. 11.)	Barnwell, Cambs.	Slade Colln. 171
3. Bottle, square, deep bluish-green; contained cremated bones; later first or second century. With 40.10—15.2 below. (Pl. 12.)	Box Lane, Hemel Hempstead, Herts.	40.10—15.1
4. Bottle, deep bluish-green, cylindrical; later first or second century. (Pl. 12.) (3, 4, cf. small jugs of similar form.)	Colchester.	81.2—3.1
5. Bowl, pillar-moulded, blue and white marbled, from grave, mid-first century. (Pl. 11.)	Radnage, Bucks.	1923.6—5.1
6. Bowl bluish-green, from grave. (Pl. 12.)	Faversham, Kent.	1312.70

FIG. 19. Metal Vessels (II, c). p. 42

7. Cup, greenish, with mould-blown
ornament commemorating victory
of Cresces in chariot race. Probably
from a factory in the Rhône valley
or Switzerland, mid-first century.
(Pl. 11.)   Colchester.   70.2—24.3

8. Flagon, pale bluish-green, from a
grave, late second or third century.
(Pl. 11.)   Bayford, Kent.   83.12—13.295

9. Flagon, pale olive green, from a
grave, early second century. (Pl.
11.)   Bayford, Kent.   83.12—13.319

10. Flagon, green, found with lead
coffin, late second century. (Pl. 12.)   Bexhill,   83.12—13.227
                                          Kent.

11. Flagon, bluish-green, late first or
early second century; from a grave.
(Pl. 12.)   Barnwell, Cambs.   Slade Colln.
                                                                 264

12. Flask, yellowish-buff. (Pl. 12.)   Chester.   1936.6—11.23

13. Flask, bluish-green. (Pl. 12.)   Southwark.   63.9—16.1

14. Oil-flask: dark blue with white   Near   1932.3—14.1
blobs; probably with a Samian   Richborough,
form 27 cup stamped IVSTI.   Kent.
Probably the South Gaulish potter
Justus who was active during the
Flavian period. (Pl. 11.)

15. Unguent bottle, colourless, found   Colchester.   44.2—23.25
in lead coffin, fourth century. (Pl.
12.)

16. Unguent bottle, bluish-green; first   Colchester.   54.4—12.22
century. (Pl. 12.)

17. Urn, globular, dark green; con-   With 40.10—15.1   40.10—15.2
tained cremated bones; later first   above.
or second century. (Pl. 12.)

A piece worth special mention is the green barrel-jug (1922.5—12.1)
from Faversham, Kent, inscribed FELIX FECIT ('made by Felix');
third century.

(e) Lamps (Fig. 20)

Roman lamps were sometimes elaborate and made with several
nozzles, but those in the collection are all relatively simple. They were
filled with oil, and a wick was inserted in the nozzle.

1. Pottery; volutes at nozzle (first-cen-   Colchester.   70.4—2.691
tury type); and relief of galley.

2. Pottery; heart-shaped nozzle   London.   94.9—26.8
(second century +); relief of
hound chasing deer.

3. Bronze, with volutes.   Hod Hill, Dorset.   92.9—1.483

$\frac{3}{5}$

14   $\frac{1}{2}$

2   $\frac{2}{5}$

7   $\frac{1}{2}$

8   $\frac{1}{5}$ 9

XI. GLASS VESSELS (II, *d*) pp. 42, 44

6 $\frac{1}{4}$

13   15 $\frac{1}{6}$ 16   12

10 $\frac{1}{4}$ 11 $\frac{1}{5}$ 3 $\frac{1}{6}$

4 $\frac{1}{8}$ 17 $\frac{1}{8}$ 1 $\frac{1}{10}$

XII. GLASS VESSELS (II, *d*) pp. 42, 44

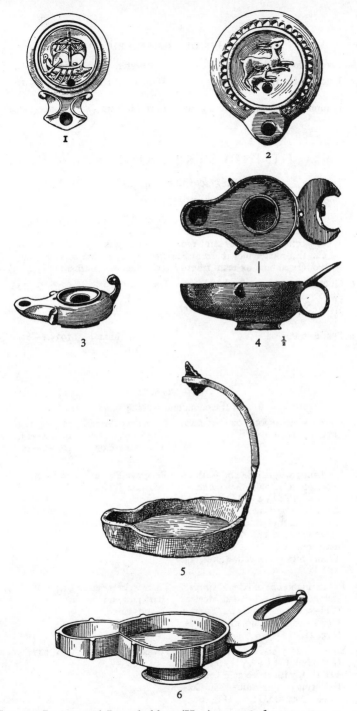

FIG. 20. Lamps and Lampholders (II, *e*). 1, 3–6: $\frac{1}{3}$; 2: $\frac{1}{2}$. pp. 44, 46

46 ANTIQUITIES OF ROMAN BRITAIN

4. Bronze, from a burial. (Fig. 20.)   Colchester.   1955.10—7.2

5. Lampholder, iron, from villa.   Wittenham Hill,   62.7—19.1
    Berks.

6. Lampholder, bronze, from a grave.   Bayford, Kent.   83.12—13.297

III. INDUSTRY AND TRADE

(a) *Agriculture* (Fig. 21)

(see Introduction)

1. Coulter, iron, from villa.   Great Witcombe,   19.3—13.1
    Glos.
    Cf. second specimen of same type, find-place unknown (1935.12—18.1).
    Cf. also model plough from Sussex (IX, *a*, 4) and bronze group of
    ploughman and ox-team from Piercebridge, Co. Durham (IV, *a*, 13).

2. Quern; an unusually large and   Ham, near Poole.   92.9—1.1755
elaborate example, made of stone
from Niedermendig, on the River
Rhine.

3. Spade-shoe, iron.   Runcton Holme,   1935.1—8.1
    Norfolk.

(b) *Metalworking*

(see Introduction, 'Mining')

1. Four copper ingots, one stamped   From Parys Mines,   72.3—9.1, 2
ME or MF, one IVES.   Anglesey, and   1906.4—14.1
    found there or in   1907.6—19.2
    N. Wales.

2. Lead pig; weight 184 lb. With an   Hexgrave Pk., nr.   79.7—2.1
inscription giving the name of   Mansfield, Notts.
GAIVS IVLIVS PROTVS, and
describing the pig as British lead
from the Lutudarum mines (probably near Matlock), with the silver
extracted. One of a number of
similar pigs in the collection. (Fig.
21.)

3. Pewter ingot, one of several similar,   Thames, between   91.2—17.1
stamped with Christian devices   Battersea and
(Chi-Rho monogram and 'Spes in   Wandsworth.
Deo') and the mark of Syagrius.
(Fig. 21.)

4. Silver ingot; stamped EX OF-   Tower of London.   O.A. 247
(FICINA) FL(AVII) HON-
ORINI, with three gold coins of
Honorius and Arcadius. (Cf. Col-
eraine Treasure, II, *c*.) (Fig. 21.)

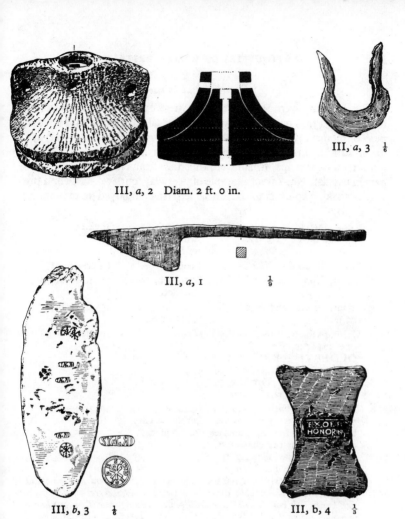

III, *a*, 2   Diam. 2 ft. 0 in.

III, *a*, 3   ⅛

III, *a*, 1   ⅑

III, *b*, 3   ⅛

III, *b*, 4   ⅓

III, *b*, 2   ⅛

FIG. 21. Agriculture and Metalworking (III, *a* and III, *b*). p. 46

(c) Reading and Writing

The Romans were accustomed to write either with sharp-pointed metal 'styli' (3, 4) on wax-surfaced wooden tablets (5), or with split-nib pens of modern type (2) and ink on papyrus or parchment (see II, *a*, 12 for a Roman inkpot). Lengthy documents and literary works were written on long strips, which were rolled up from either end leaving the part in use flat. No. 1 is an example of everyday 'cursive' script and provides a striking contrast to the formal lettering employed on monuments (cf. VI, b).

1. Curse, incised in cursive script on lead tablet. (Fig. 22.) — Telegraph St., Moorgate, City of London. — 1934.11—5.1

2. Pen, split, bronze. (Fig. 22.) — London. — 65.12—20.21

3. Stylus, iron, stamped REGN F. (Fig. 22.) — Walbrook, London. — 1934.12—10.78

4. Stylus, bronze and iron. (Fig. 22.) — Old Jewry, City of London. — 1934.11—6.3

5. Writing tablets, three, wooden; one branded PROC AVG DEDERVNT/BRIT PROV ('Issued by the Imperial Procurators of the Province of Britain.') (Fig. 22.) — Walbrook, London. — 1934.12—10.98–100

6. Three wooden writing tablets, probably first century. One has LONDINIO inscribed on the outside in cursive characters. On the inside the following cursive inscription has been impressed through the original wax coating; *Rufus callisuni salutem epillico et omnibus contubernalibus certiores vos esse credo me recte valere si vos indicem fecistis rogo mittite omnia diligenter cura agas ut illam puellam ad nummum redigas* . . . 'Rufus, son of Callisunus, greeting to Epillicus and all his fellows. I believe you know I am very well. If you have made the list, please send. Do thou look after everything carefully. See that thou turnest that slave-girl into cash. . . .' — Walbrook, Lothbury, City of London. — 1953.10—2.1–3

(d) Textiles

No. 4 is characteristic Romano-British type of spindle-whorl; such whorls were mounted like miniature fly-wheels on the spindle to give additional momentum while spinning thread. This particular type of lead whorl with dot and line relief ornament is fairly common on Romano-British sites, and one (57.11—13.19) was found in positive association with Romano-British material at Dowkerbottom Cave, Yorks.

1. Bone plates, triangular, with three perforations; used in weaving. (Fig. 23.) — Bank of England. — 1928.7—13.15

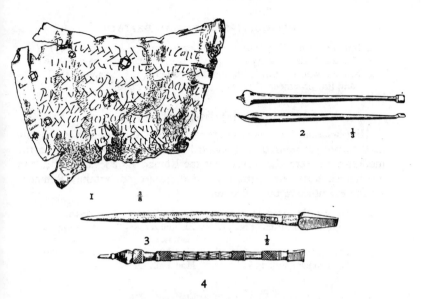

FIG. 22. Reading and Writing (III, *c*). p. 48

(*III, c, 1 after R. G. Collingwood in 'Journal of Roman Studies', vol. xxv.*)

2. Spindle, wood. (Fig. 23.) London. 56.7—1.1071
3. Spindle, bone. (Fig. 23.) Bank of England. 1928.7—13.26
4. Spindle-whorl, lead, with dot Woodhouse, 83.7—5.110
   and line ornament. (Fig. 23.) Northumberland.

(e) Transport

'Hippo-sandals' (2) were a temporary form of shoe for horses, possibly used to protect injured or diseased limbs. Horse-shoes similar to the modern type were also in use, but the Roman varieties are difficult to distinguish from later patterns, and there are no certainly Romano-British examples in the collection.

1. Chariot-fitting, iron. (Fig. 23.) Sandy, Beds. 1915.12—8.334
2. 'Hippo-sandal', iron. (Fig. 23.) Bishopsgate, 71.7—14.22
   London.
3. Ox-shoe, iron. (Fig. 23.) Hod Hill, Dorset. 93.6—1.129
4. Spur, bronze. (Fig. 23.) Hod Hill, Dorset. 92.9—1.495

(f) Various Industrial, &c.

The Kimmeridge shale industry began in the Early Iron Age, and continued to flourish after the Roman conquest. The shale was worked in the vicinity of the outcrops, and made into bracelets, decorative panels, and other ornamental objects. The industry is of particular interest as exemplifying the use of the lathe, and also the survival of primitive equipment, namely the flint chisels used for turning.

Fly-wheels such as (1) and (2) may come from lathes or possibly potters' wheels.

Fly-wheels

1. Chalk, 2. Hod Hill, Dorset. 93.6—1.1, 2
2. Shale. Kimmeridge, 1940.7—1.1034
   Dorset.

Shale Industry

3. Waste disk of shale. (Fig. 24.) Kimmeridge, 1937.12—7.55
   Dorset.
4. Flint chisels, 2. (Fig. 24.) Kimmeridge, 1937.12—7.65,66
   Dorset

Iron Tools, Various

5. Axe. (Fig. 24.) Glos. 10.2—10.5/6
6. Crowbar; first century. (Fig. 24.) Walbrook, City of 1955.11—8.1
   London.
7. Gouge-bit. (Fig. 24.) Bucklebury, 93.7—15.7
   Berks.
8. Knife, with ornamental bone London. 56.7—1.1118
   handle. (Fig. 24.)

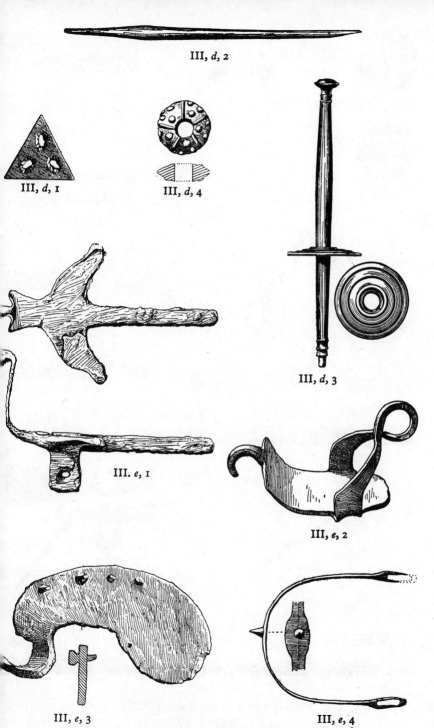

III, *d*, 2

III, *d*, 1

III, *d*, 4

III, *d*, 3

III. *e*, 1

III, *e*, 2

III, *e*, 3

III, *e*, 4

FIG. 23. Textiles and Transport (III, *d* and III, *e*). III, *d*, 1–4: ½;
III, *e*, 1–2: ¼; 3 and 4: ½. pp. 48, 50

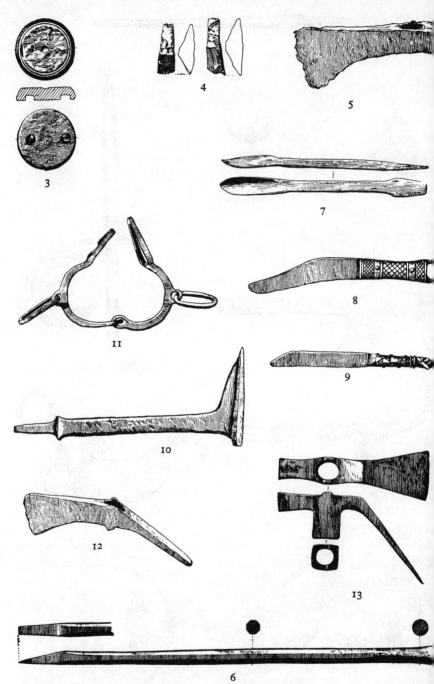

FIG. 24. Shale-working and Iron Implements (III, *f*). 3, 4, 7–9, 11: ⅓;
5, 10, 12, 13: ⅙. pp. 50, 53

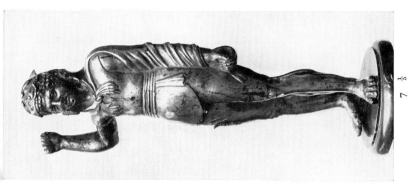

1 ⅓

7 ⅕

XIII. BRONZE FIGURES (IV, *a*) p. 54

12 $\frac{1}{5}$

11 $\frac{2}{5}$

XIV. BRONZE FIGURES (IV, a) p. 54

9. Knife, with bronze handle engraved with triangular pattern; handle ornamented with steel studs and with lion's head terminal. (Fig. 24.) — Walbrook, London. — 1934.12—10.42
10. Last. (Fig. 24.) — Sandy, Beds. — 1915.12—8.329
11. Manacle. (Fig. 24.) — Walbrook, London. — 1934.12—10.88
12. Mattock. (Fig. 24.) — Hod Hill, Dorset. — 92.9—1.1259
13. Adze-hammer; first century. (Fig. 24.) — Bull's Wharf, City of London. — 1956.4—3.1

IV. ART

(a) *Bronze Figures,* and (b) *Stone Sculptures*

The two main forces actuating plastic art in Roman Britain are exemplified by pieces selected from the collection for illustration. On the one hand is the classical naturalism introduced by the Romans, shown in figures of deities and emperors such as the Barking Hall Nero (IV, *a,* 12), the group from London Bridge (IV, *a,* 17), or, with a secular subject, the Cheapside Archer (IV, *a,* 1). Work of this kind varies from

5   7

FIG. 25. Stone Sculptures (IV, *b*). ⅓. p. 55

such proficient if uninspired pieces as those just quoted, through second-rate figures such as the Spoonley Wood Bacchus (IV, *b,* 10) and the Lincoln relief (IV, *b,* 3) to poor and spiritless provincial copy-work.

In spite of the official approbation of naturalism, the native tradition was still sometimes able to produce such masterpieces of abstract but powerful formalism as the Towcester Antefix (IV, *b,* 1); the relief from Wellow (IV, *b,* 6) is a lesser example of such Romano-British art, though in a different style.

Finally, there are minor pieces of native work, often revealing to the archaeologist, the individual character of which deserves our notice. Such are the Captives from Brough and London (IV, *a*, 2, 3), the Piercebridge group (IV, *a*, 13), and the Deities from Southbroom (IV, *a*, 16).

(*a*) Bronze Figures

1. Archer. (Pl. 13.)	Cheapside, London	82.5—18.1
2. Captive. (Pl. 15.)	Brough, Westm'l'd.	74.3—28.42
3. Captive. (Pl. 15.)	London.	56.7—1.20
4. Gladiator. (Pl. 15.)	?	88.7—19.97
5. Hadrian, colossal head. (Pl. 15.)	Thames, London Bridge.	48.11—3.1

Cf. arm from same figure, found in Lower Thames Street (56.7—1.18).

6. Harpocrates (silver). (Pl. 15.)	London Bridge.	25.11—12
7. Hercules, gilt. (Pl. 13.)	Hadrian's Wall, probably near Birdoswald.	95.4—8.1
8. Jupiter. (Pl. 16.)	Earith, Hunts.	71.6—1
9. Jupiter (restored). (Pl. 16.)	Ranksborough Hill, Rutland.	91.12—13.2
10. Mars, found with silver votive plaques, &c. (Pl. 16.)	Barkway, Herts.	17.3—8
11. Mars, with inscription which may be translated: 'To the God Mars and the Imperial Divinities, the Colasuni, Bruccius, and Caratius offered 100 sesterces from their own purse; Celatus the copper-smith made the figure and contributed a pound of bronze made at a cost of 3 denarii.' (Pl. 14.)	Fossdyke, at Torksey, Lincs.	O.A. 248
12. Nero. (Pl. 14.)	Barking Hall, Suffolk.	13.2—13
13. Ploughman, with ox-team. (Pl. 16.)	Piercebridge, Co. Durham.	79.7—10.1
14. Lamp or oil-flask in form of sleeping slave. (Pl. 18.)	Aldborough, Yorks.	Payne Knight Colln., 1824
15. Venus. (Pl. 18.)	Colchester.	70.7—15.1
16. Barbaric group of classical deities. (Pl. 17.)	Southbroom, Wilts.	11.3—9
17. Group of four figures, ? intentionally damaged:	Thames, London Bridge.	
Apollo. (Pl. 17.)		56.7—1.14
Ganymede. (Pl. 17.)		48.8—3.44
Mercury. (Pl. 17.)		56.7—1.15
Jupiter (damaged).		56.7—1.16

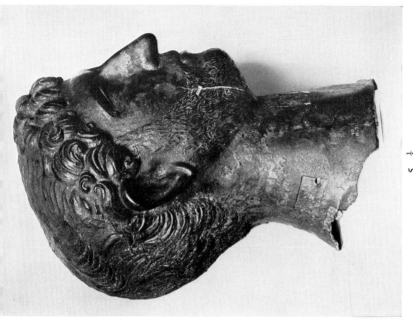

3 $\frac{1}{1}$

2 $\frac{1}{1}$

5 $\frac{1}{4}$

6 $\frac{3}{2}$

4 $\frac{3}{2}$

XV. BRONZE FIGURES (IV, a) p. 54

8 $\frac{1}{3}$

10 $\frac{1}{3}$

9 $\frac{1}{4}$

13 $\frac{1}{1}$

XVI. BRONZE FIGURES (IV, a) p. 54

(b) *Stone Sculptures*

1. Funerary head.   Towcester,   O.A. 249
   Northants.
2. Relief, standard with goat and Pegasus   Hadrian's Wall,   O.A. 250
  badges of the 2nd Legion 'Augusta'.   at Benwell,
  (Pl. 19.)   Northumberland
3. Relief, Mother-Goddesses. (Pl. 19.)   Lincoln.   56.5—7
4. Reliefs of the deities of the days of the   Chesterford,   Don. p. 48
  week, carved on a stone half-octagon.   Essex.
  (Pl. 19.)

IV, *b*, 1   ⅛   p. 55

5. Relief, barbaric hooded and cloaked   Rushall Down,   1902.6—16.79
  figure. From R.B. settlement. (Fig.   Wilts.
  25).
6. Relief, three figures, two women and   Wellow, Som.   52.4—22.1
  ? Mercury. (Pl. 19.)
7. Sculpture, circular face and conven-   Charterhouse-   1939.3—5.1
  tional features. (Fig. 25.)   on-Mendip,
   Blagdon, Som.
8. Statue, head only, marble. (Pl. 20.)   Nr. Colchester.   1935.1—12.1
9. Statue of Atys in oolite. (Pl. 20.)   City of London.   56.7—1.1
10. Statue of Bacchus in marble, from   Spoonley Wood,   1910.6—25
  grave. (Pl. 20.)   nr. Winch-
   combe, Glos.
11. Statue of Luna in marble from the villa.   Woodchester,   11.6—7
  (Pl. 20.)   Glos.

(c) Minor Arts

Enamel

1. Casket (replica); blue, green, and red; from grave. (Pl. 21.) — Bartlow Hills, Essex. —
2. Cup, green and blue. (Pl. 21.) — Braughing, Herts. — 70.12—1.1
3. Plaque in form of altar; blue, red, and light-green; pelta motives, pair of gryphons and pair of lions, each flanking a vase. (Pl. 21.) — Thames. — 56.7—1.1380

Niello

4. Items of military equipment (buckles and a pendant); bronze, tinned or silvered and inlaid with niello. From the Roman fort, first century A.D. (Pl. 17.) — Hod Hill, Dorset. — 92.9—1, 803, 838, 857.

FIG. 26. Jet and Shale Carvings (IV, c). ½. p. 56

Millefiori

5. Bronze enamelled stud, from Roman fort; fourth century. (Pl. 21.) — Chesterholm, North'l'd. — 1938.4—3.1
6. Bronze enamelled plate. (Pl. 21.) — Nr. Chepstow, Mon. — 91.3—27.9

Jet

7. Carving, two cupids, from burial. (Fig. 26.) — Colchester. — 52.6—26.1

Shale

8. Carving, lion, from Roman building. (Fig. 26.) — Jordan Hill, Weymouth. — 92.9—1.1727

V. ARCHITECTURE
(a) General

Some of the characteristic varieties of tiles used by Roman builders in Britain are detailed below (3–7). (3) is a decorated flue tile, used for conducting the hot gases from a hypocaust (see Introduction) through the walls of a building. Such tiles usually have their faces scored, or made uneven by an impressed design, in order to give a firm hold to the

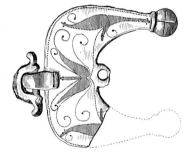

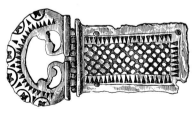

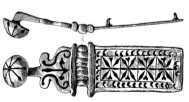

17 $\frac{1}{3}$

16 $\frac{1}{3}$

$\frac{3}{4}$

$\frac{1}{2}$

$\frac{3}{5}$

XVII. BRONZE FIGURES (IV, *a*)   p. 54

OBJECTS WITH NIELLO ORNAMENT (IV, *c*, 4) p. 56

II, c, 6 $\frac{5}{8}$

IV, a, 15 $\frac{3}{5}$

II, c, 4 $\frac{1}{4}$

IV, a, 14 $\frac{1}{2}$

XVIII. METAL VESSELS (II, c, 4 and 6)   p. 38
BRONZE FIGURES (IV, a, 14 and 15)   p. 54

6 ⅙

3 ⅕

2 ⅕

4 Length 47 ins.

XIX. STONE SCULPTURES (IV, b)   p. 55

8 $\frac{3}{7}$

9 $\frac{1}{9}$

10 $\frac{1}{7}$

11 $\frac{1}{5}$

XX. STONE SCULPTURES (IV, b) p. 55

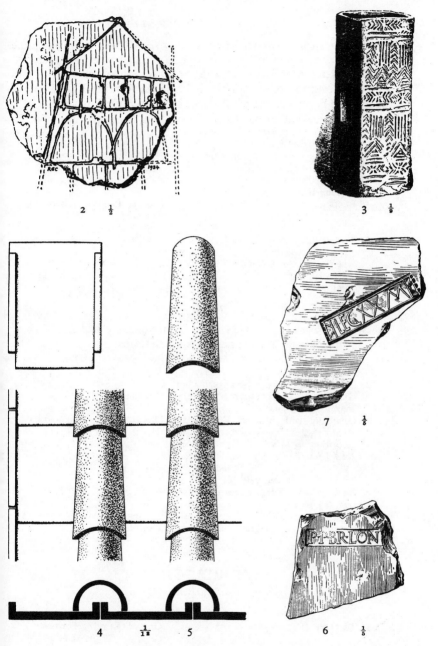

2 ½   3 ⅑

4   1/12 5   7 ⅛   6 ⅕

FIG. 27. Architecture (V, a). p. 58
(V, a, 2 after R. G. Collingwood in 'Journal of Roman Studies', vol. xxiv.)

5

wall-plaster which covered them. Fig. 27 shows the way in which the
'tegula' (4) and 'imbrex' (5) were used to obtain a watertight roof.

The sketch of a house scratched on a piece of plaster (2) provides
valuable evidence of the way in which larger Romano-British houses
may have been constructed; it shows a 'half-timbered' technique.

1. Antefix (ornament for the apex of a   Holt, Denbighs.   1911.2—6
   gable), pottery, with boar crest of 20th
   Legion. (Cover.)
2. Plaster, incised with drawing of a   Hucclecote,   1939.6—2.2
   house; from a villa. (Fig. 27.)   Glos.
3. Decorated flue-tile. (Fig. 27.)   Reigate, Surrey. 52.4—19.1
4. Roofing-tile, 'tegula'. (Fig. 27.)   ?   61.3—1.2
5. Roofing tile, 'imbrex'. (Fig. 27.)   Pudding Pan   1909.11—9.2
                                            Rock, Herne
                                            Bay, Kent.
6. Tile, stamped P. P. BR. LON ('Pub-   London.   56.7—1.717
   licani ("tax-gatherers") of London in
   the Province of Britain.') (Fig. 27.)
7. Tile, with stamp of 20th Legion. (Fig. Chester.   55.9—11.1
   27.)

(b) Mosaics

Mosaic pavements such as those illustrated were laid in the chief
rooms of villas and of large buildings in the towns.

1. Chariot race; from a villa; fourth cen- Horkstow,   Dep. p. 27
   tury? (Pl. 22.)   Lincs.
2. Bacchus riding on panther; ornamental   Leadenhall St.,   O.A. 290
   border. The illustration shows the   London.
   pavement restored. (Pl. 22.)
3. Originally with head of Bacchus in   Thruxton,   99.6—14.1
   centre; heads of Seasons at corners; in- Hants.
   scription QVINTVS NATALIVS
   NATALINVS ET BODENI/...
   V...O. From a villa. Dated by coins
   to mid-fourth century. (Pl. 23.)
4. Oceanus, with dolphins, sea-monsters,   Withington,   Don. p. 51
   &c. (Pl. 23.)   Glos.
5. Border of dolphins and mullet sur-   Hemsworth,   1908.12—15.1
   rounding a damaged representation of   Dorset.
   Venus rising from the sea.

VI. RELIGION
(see Introduction)
(a) Altars

1. To Mars. (Fig. 28.)   King's Stanley,   Towneley
                                            Glos.   Colln.

Some of the inscriptions on other altars in the collection are of particular interest. 56.7—1.5026 from Lympne, Kent, has a dedication to

3 $\frac{1}{2}$

2 $\frac{2}{5}$

I $\frac{1}{4}$

6 $\frac{3}{5}$

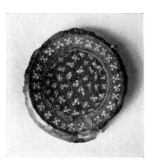

5 $\frac{3}{4}$

XXI. MINOR ARTS (IV, c) p. 56

1. Length: 19 ft. 5 in.

2. Diam. of medallion: 2 ft. 8¼ in.

XXII. MOSAICS (V, *b*)   p. 58

VI, *a*, 1 Ht. 1 ft. 11½ in.

VI, *b*, 1 Height 7 ft.

VI, *b*, 2 Ht. 4 ft. 6 in.

VI, *b*. 3 Ht. 4 ft. 11 in.

FIG. 28. Altar and Tombstones (VI, *a* and VI, *b*). pp. 58, 60

Neptune by G. Aufidius Pantera, commander of the British Fleet. The dedication of 68.10—4.1 (from Old Penrith, Cumberland) to Mars Belatucader shows the identification of a native deity with the Roman god of war. 56.7—1.5025, from Winchester, is dedicated to the Mother Goddesses of Italy, Germany, Gaul, and Britain.

(b) Tombstones

Tombstones may well be considered under the general heading of religion, since they are usually dedicated 'to the Gods of the Underworld' (*Dis Manibus*, often abbreviated to D.M.).

1. To Gaius Saufeius, a soldier of the 9th Legion who died aged 40 after 22 years' service. (Fig. 28.) — Lincoln. — 73.5—21.1
2. Erected by Aurelius Senecio to his wife Volusia Faustina of Lincoln. (Fig. 28.) — Lincoln. — 62.4—23.1
3. To Titus Valerius Pudens, of the 2nd Legion 'Adiutrix'; with trident, dolphins, and pioneer's mattock. (Fig. 28.) — Lincoln. — 53.11—8
4. To Gaius Valerius Victor, standard-bearer of the 2nd Legion 'Augusta'. (Fig. 29.) — Caerleon. — O.A. 251
5. To Julius Classicianus, procurator of Britain, 61–c. 65. (Fig. 29.) — Trinity Ho. Sq. and Trinity Place, London. — 52.8—6.2 1935.7—12.1

(c) Various

1. Bronze instrument; two bars originally hinged at one end; heads of deities along outer edges, inner edges serrated. Probably a clamp used for ritual mutilation by the worshippers of Cybele. (Pl. 24.) — Thames, London Bridge. — 56.7—1.33
2. Bronzes (Pl. 24.): — Felmingham Hall, Norfolk. — 1925.6—10

   (i) Head of bearded god (1925.6—10.1)
   (ii)   ,,   Minerva (,, 2)
   (iii) ,,   Helioserapis (,, 3)
   (iv) Statuette of a Lar (,, 4)
   (v) Figure of a bird (,, 7)
   (vi)   ,,   ,, (,, 8)
   (vii) Wheel (,, 9)
   (viii) Mount with mask, one of three (,, 16)
   (ix) Pole-tip (,, 23)

Also two pedestals, two patera-handles, various ornamental mounts, &c., and silver coin of Valerian (255–9). All contained in a pot with

3. Height: 14 ft. 9 in.

4. Length: 12 ft. 2 in.

XXIII. MOSAICS (v, *b*)   p. 58

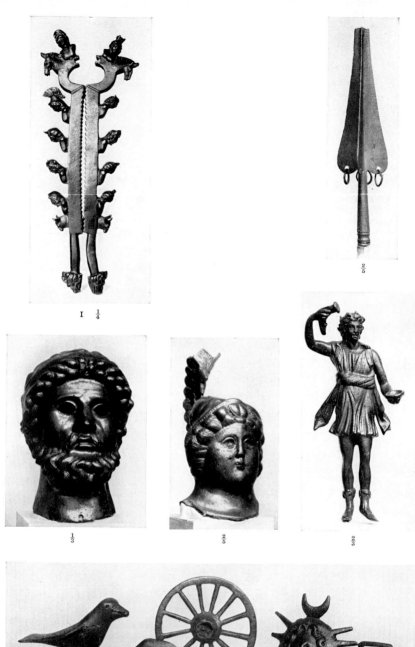

I   ¼

⅖

⅓

⅖

⅔

2   ½

XXIV. RELIGIOUS OBJECTS (VI, c)   p. 60

4. L. 3 ft. 11 in.

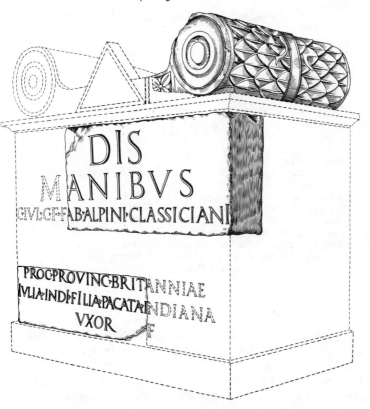

5. L. about 7 ft. 6 in.

FIG. 29. Tombstones (VI, *b*). p. 60

ring-handles (II, *b*, 29), with other coarse pottery. A votive deposit or a priest's cache.

3. Leaden tank, cylindrical, with Early Christian Chi-Rho and Alpha/Omega symbols; found near a villa. Perhaps a font. (Fig. 30.)	Icklingham, Suffolk.	1946.2—4.1
4. Bronze votive tablet, inscribed with a dedication to Mars and the Emperor Alexander Severus (222–35). The dedicator is described as 'Caledo'; it is not certain whether this is a proper name, or means 'a Caledonian'. (Fig. 30.)	Colchester.	92.4—21.1
5. Pipeclay figure of Venus, head missing. (Fig. 30.)	Minories, London.	54.11—30.42
6. Head of pipeclay figure, probably of a maternity goddess. (Fig. 30.)	Rawreth, Essex.	56.7—1.5108
7. Pipeclay figure of bird. (Fig. 30.)	Colchester.	70.4—2.466
8. Sceptre-binding, bronze; embossed with stylized animal and human forms; from a Romano-Celtic temple. The figures probably represent Celtic deities. (Fig. 31.)	Farley Heath, Surrey.	1936.3—11.1
9. Votive plaques, silver; dedicated to Mars and Vulcan. Found with a statuette of Mars (IV, *a*, 10) and bronze patera-handle. Three selected specimens only are shown. (Fig. 31.)	Barkway, Herts.	17.3—8

Cf. similar plaques, dedicated to various deities, from Stony Stratford, Bucks. (O.A. 252.)

10. Five diadems and a 'crown', all of sheet-bronze; probably priests' regalia. The diadems bear silver plaques with repoussé designs representing either a	Hockwold-cum-Wilton, Norfolk.	1956.10—11.1-3 1957.2—6.1-3

barbarous form of the classical vase-and-two birds motive, or a crudely-rendered male human figure holding a crook-like object and a sphere. (The 'crown' and one diadem are illustrated on Pl. 25.)

VII. BURIAL

Roman law forbade the burial of the dead within the limits of a town and tombs are commonly to be found along the roads just outside centres of population. The lead canister (1) and porphyry urn (6) from Warwick Square were found just within the wall of Roman London, and are interesting as evidence that the boundary had not been delimited at the time of their deposition. At first cremation was the normal rite, but during the third century it gave way to inhumation, partly, no doubt, as a result of the spread of Christianity. Offerings, utensils, and other goods are often found in pagan graves. Where cremation was practised, the

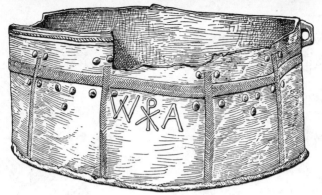

3   Diam. 2 ft. 8 in.

DEO·MARTI·MEDOCIO·CAMP
ESIVM·TT·VICTORIE·ALEXAN
DRI·PII·FELICIS·AVGVSTI·NOSI
DONVM·LOSSIO·VEDA·DE·SVO
POSVIT·NEPO·SVEPOCENICEDO

4   ⅛

6   ½

5   ⅜   7   ¼

FIG. 30. Objects of Religious Use (VI, c). p. 62

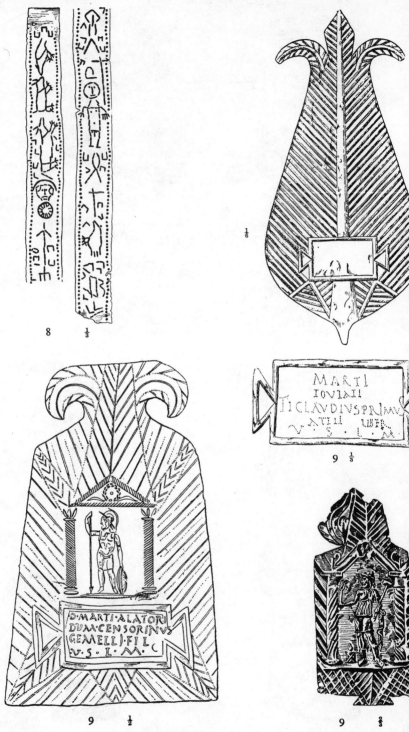

8   ⅓

⅛

9   ⅓

MARTI
IOVINII
TICLAVDINSPRIMV
ᴠ·ATILI·VBER·
S · L · M

9   ½

D·MARTI·ALATOR
DVM·CENSORINVS
GEMELLI·FIL
ᴠ·S·L·M·

9   ⅜

FIG. 31. Objects of Religious Use (VI, *c*). p. 62

1 Ht. 1 ft. 1¾ in.

6   ⅐

2 L. 4 ft. 3 in.   3 L. 5 ft. 0 in.   4 L. 4 ft. 6 in.

FIG. 32. Burial (VII). p. 66

ashes were often buried in pottery jars (e.g. II, *b*, 5, 6) or glass vessels like II, *d*, 1, 3, 4 and 17.

1. Canister, lead, with figure of Sol in chariot; contained glass cinerary urn. (Fig. 32.) — Warwick Sq., London. — Dep. p. 7

2.*Coffin, lead with cable pattern, &c.; contained skeleton of child, bracelets and third-century gold ring; originally encased in wood; accompanied by pottery and glass vessels. (Fig. 32.) — Watling St., nr. Sitting-bourne, Kent. — 83.12—13.374

3. Coffin, lead, originally encased in wood; bead-and-reel decoration, also Medusa medallions, and pairs of lions, flanking vases containing torches. (Fig. 32.) — Milton-next-Sittingbourne, Kent. — 83.12—13.619

4. Coffin, lead, bead-and-reel and scallop-shell ornament. Found in 5. (Fig. 32.) — 53.6—20.2

FIG. 33. Sarcophagus from the Minories, London (VII, 5).
L. 5 ft. 0 in.　p. 66

5. Coffin, stone, carved. (Fig. 33.) — Minories, London. — 53.6—20.1

6. Urn, cinerary, porphyry, contained coin of Claudius. (Fig. 32.) — Warwick Sq., London. — Dep. p. 6

VIII. WAR

(*a*) *Armour*

The Guisborough (3) and Ribchester (4) helmets are respectively too fragile and too elaborate to have been used in actual combat. They were parade pieces, used in the cavalry exercises which were introduced to the Roman army by Celtic auxiliaries.

* Stolen from the Museum in November 1950.

$\frac{1}{3}$

$\frac{1}{3}$

XXV. WILTON CROWN, DIADEM AND PLAQUES (VI, *c*, 10)   p. 62

3　$\frac{1}{6}$

4　$\frac{1}{5}$

5　$\frac{1}{4}$

6
$\frac{1}{8}$

XXVI. HELMETS
(VIII, *a*)
p. 67

1. Armour, chain, late first century.	Chester.	1928.7—9.8
2. Armour, scale, found with coins of Hadrian.	Chester.	1928.7—9.4–7
3. Helmet, thin 'gilding metal' (i.e. brass with low zinc content); repoussé and chased ornament, figures of Mars, Minerva, and Victory on front, also serpents. Late third century? (Pl. 26.)	Guisborough, Yorks.	78.9—10.1
4. Helmet, bronze, with vizor-mask; crown embossed with combat scenes, mask topped with mural crown and figures in relief. First or early second century. (Pl. 26.)	Ribchester, Lancs.	Towneley Colln.
5. Helmet, bronze: a standard first-century legionary pattern. At each side is a plume-holder and the attachment for a cheek-piece. Four inscriptions on the neck-guard give the names of successive owners. (Pl. 26.)	London.	1950.7—6
6. Helmet, bronze, with separate front, cheek-pieces, and neck-guard. (Pl. 26.)	Witcham Gravel, Ely.	91.11—17.1
7. Shield-boss, bronze, with incised ornament; Mars? in centre, shield-trophies, eagles, and human figures on rim. (Fig. 34.)	Kirkham, Lancs.	Towneley Colln.
8. Shield-boss, bronze; ornamented with figures reserved against niello ground, four Seasons, Mars, Bull, Eagle (on	River Tyne.	93.12—13.1

boss): also two standards. Pounced inscription: LEG VIII AVG (8th Legion 'Augusta', whose badge was the bull), and ƆIVL MAGNI IVNI DVBITATI, i.e. (The property of) Junius Dubitatus, of Julius Magnus' company. A detachment of the 8th Legion served in Britain under Hadrian. (Fig. 35.)

(b) Weapons (Fig. 36)

The standard weapons of the Roman legionaries who conquered Britain were the *gladius*, or short sword (5), and *pilum*. The latter was a throwing spear with wooden shaft, and a long slender iron forepart terminating in a small head; no complete example of such irons is included in the collection. The head of a catapult dart (1) is representative of Roman artillery, of which there were two principal types. The first, the *catapulta* (firing darts) and *ballista* (firing stone missiles), was somewhat similar to a greatly enlarged crossbow. Power was provided by two twists of gut or horsehair, mounted vertically at each side. Through each of these an arm was passed horizontally, and the ends of the 'bowstring' were attached to these. In the second type a bundle of hair or gut was mounted horizontally, and the missile was launched from a long arm swinging vertically; such a weapon was called an *onager*, or donkey, because of its kick.

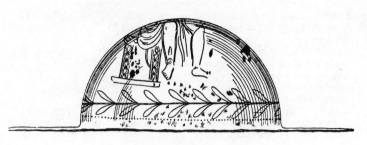

FIG. 34. Shield-boss from Kirkham, Lancs.
(VIII, *a*, 7). ½. p. 67

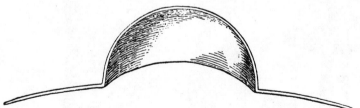

FIG. 35. Shield-centre from the River Tyne (VIII, *a*, 8). $\frac{2}{5}$.
p. 67

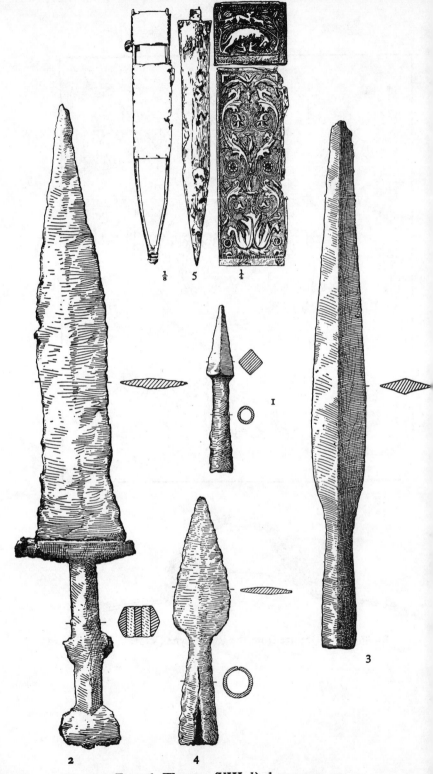

$\frac{1}{8}$ 5 $\frac{1}{4}$

1

3

2   4

FIG. 36. Weapons (VIII, *b*). $\frac{1}{2}$ exc. 5. p. 71

1. Catapult-dart (iron head only).	Hod Hill, Dorset.	92.9—1.1141
2. Dagger, iron.	Hod Hill, Dorset.	92.9—1.1210
3. Spearhead, iron. (Fig. 36.)	Hod Hill, Dorset.	92.9—1.1015
4. Spearhead, iron.	Hod Hill, Dorset.	92.9—1.1033
5. Sword, iron, with embossed bronze scabbard ornamented with a scroll design and the wolf suckling Romulus and Remus.	Thames, Fulham.	83.4—7.1

(c) Diplomas

These interesting and informative documents were issued by the Emperor to time-expired auxiliary soldiers, and conferred the rights of citizenship and legal marriage. Each diploma is in the form of a pair of inscribed bronze plates.

| 1. Issued by Trajan in 103 to Reburrus the Spaniard, son of Severus, decurion in the 1st Pannonian cavalry regiment the Tampian, commanded by Caius Valerius Celsus, serving in Britain. | Malpas, Cheshire. | 13.12—11 (a) |

> Cf. the following Diplomas issued to troops serving in Britain: 80.7—7.1, from Chesters, Northumberland, issued in 146 by Antoninus Pius; 57.11—27, from Stannington, Yorks, issued by Hadrian in 124; 13.12—11 (b) from Sydenham Common, Kent, issued by Trajan in 105.

IX. MISCELLANEOUS
(a) Models (Fig. 37)

The group from Sussex (4) is of particular interest; these little bronzes may have been toys or amulets, or offerings to the dead or to a god. Miniature axes such as those shown here, and also axe-headed pins, are quite common in Romano-British contexts. Their presence in graves both in this country and on the Continent suggests that they were amulets; possibly they were connected with the cult of Mithras.

1. Galley-prow, bronze, with reversed inscription AMMILLA AVG FELIX.	London.	56.7—1.29
2. Shovel, bronze.	Cirencester.	1906.2—14.1
3. Stool, bronze, with red, green, and blue enamel ornament. (There are several similar specimens in the collection.)	Farley Heath, Albury, Sussex.	53.4—19.119
4. Tools (axes, mattock, saws), plough, bolts and wards of locks; bronze; from a barrow?	Sussex.	54.12—27.76–85

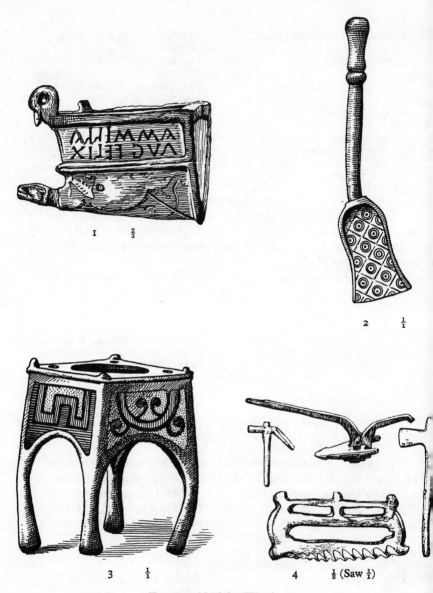

1   ⅔

2   ⅟₁

3   ⅟₁

4   ½ (Saw ¼)

Fig. 37. Models (IX, *a*). p. 71

(b) Oculists' Stamps

The example illustrated is one of several in the collection. These stamps were used to mark cakes of eye-ointment with the maker's name and the nature of the remedy.

1. Green stone; each side is inscribed with the name of the oculist (T VINDACVS ARIOVISTVS) and that of a medicament, as follows: ANICET(VM) ('Unbeatable', a preparation of aniseed or dill), NARD (VM) (spikenard), CHLORON (green salve); the name of the preparation on the fourth side is not definitely legible. These inscriptions are all reversed so as to give a positive impression. On one face SENIOR is roughly incised, on the other SENI: both are reversed. Senior was probably the name of a later owner of the stamp. (Fig. 38.)

Kenchester, Hereford.   1931.2—11.1

FIG. 38. Oculist's Stamp (IX, *b*, 1). ¼. p. 73

(c) Various

1.*Casket, lead with moulded lettering CVNOBARRVS FECIT VIVAS. Two fragments only are in the British Museum, another piece is in the Lincoln Museum. Probably fourth century; cf. the Projecta casket in the Esquiline treasure, also in the British Museum. (Fig. 39.)

Caistor, Lincs.   64.11—12

2. Counters, pottery. (Fig. 40.)

53.6—27.58   53.6—27.58, 59
comes from   65.4—8,107, 108
Gt. Chesterford, Essex;
the find-places of the
others are not known.

* The larger British Museum fragment, as illustrated, was stolen in November, 1950.

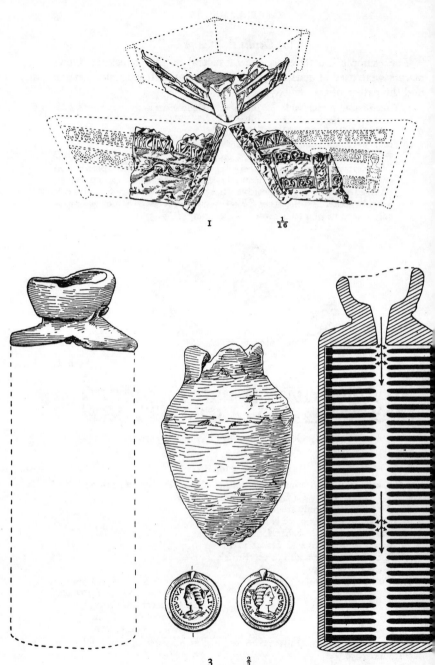

1      $\frac{1}{16}$

3    $\frac{2}{3}$

Fig. 39. Miscellaneous (IX, c). pp. 73, 78

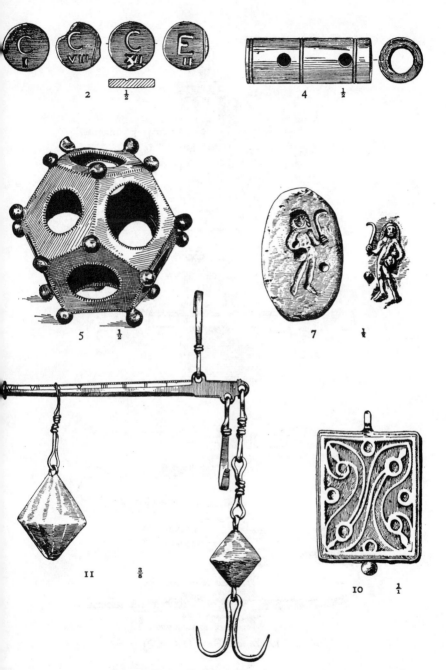

FIG. 40. Miscellaneous (IX, *c*). pp. 73, 78

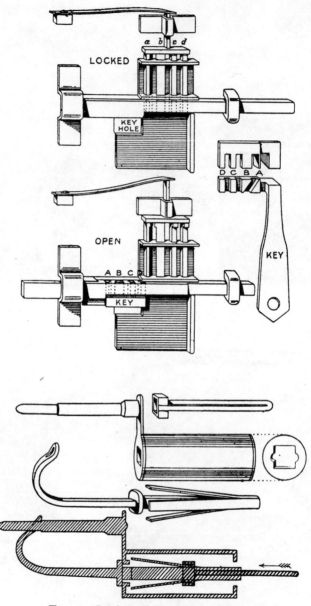

FIG. 41. Locks and Keys (IX, *c*, 8). p. 78

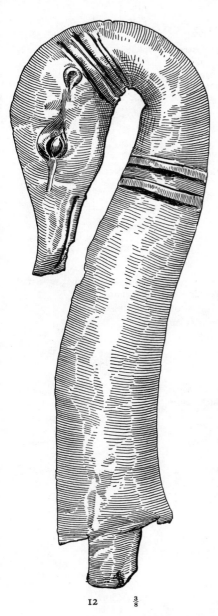

IMP·CAES·TRAI
·ANVS·HADRIA
AVG·P·M·TRI
E·P·P·COS·III
A·KANOVIO
M·P·VIII

9 Ht. 5 ft. 5 in.

12        $\frac{3}{8}$

FIG. 42. Miscellaneous (IX, c). p. 78

3. Crucible and moulds used for casting coins; the moulds shown are for denarii of Septimius Severus (193–211) and his wife Julia Domna. (Fig. 39.) — Probably from Lingwell Gate, nr. Wakefield, Yorks. — Londesborough Colln.

4. Cylinder, perforated bone; perhaps a section of a flute. (Fig. 40.) — London. — 56.7—1.1297

5. Dodecahedron, bronze. (Fig. 40.) — Fishguard, Pembroke. — 1924.4—11.1

6. Five sections of gold bar, and a gold pellet. Each piece of bar is stamped with one of the Roman numerals I to V; their weights are:
   I: approx. 14 gm.
   II: „   16 „
   III: „   26 „
   IV: „   31 „
   V: „   38 „
   — Wimborne, Dorset. — 65.4—11.1–6

7. 'Hockey-player' figure, clay mould for; from site of Roman kiln. (Fig. 40.) — Kettering, Northants. — 1939.6—4.1

8. Locks and keys. Models of two principal types of lock used in Roman Britain are shown in Fig. 41.

9. Milestone, erected by Hadrian, 8 miles from Kanovium (Caerhyn), near Conway. (Fig. 42.) — Llanfairfechan, Carnarvon. — 83.7—25.1

10. Seal-box lid, bronze, enamelled with ornament in Celtic style. Such boxes were used to protect the seal of a package during transit. (Fig. 40.) — Lincoln. — 75.6—25.3

11. Steelyard, bronze. (Fig. 40.) — Walbrook, London. — 1935.10—28.1

12. Swan- or goose-head, bronze, repoussé; perhaps a model of the *cheniscus* or large goose-head on the stern of a Roman ship; from the Roman Fort. (Fig. 42.) — Richborough, Kent. — 1950.4—2.1

SHORT BIBLIOGRAPHY

General

I. A. RICHMOND: *Roman Britain* (Penguin Books, 1955).
A. L. F. RIVET: *Town and Country in Roman Britain* (Hutchinson, 1958).
R. G. COLLINGWOOD: *Archaeology of Roman Britain* (Methuen, 1930).
R. G. COLLINGWOOD and J. N. L. MYRES: *Roman Britain and the English Settlements* (Oxford Univ. Press, 2nd ed., 1937).
I. A. RICHMOND (Ed.): *Roman and Native in North Britain* (Nelson, 1958).
M. and C. H. B. QUENNELL: *Everyday Life in Roman Britain* (Batsford, 3rd (revised) ed., 1952). Suitable for children.
Ordnance Survey: *Map of Roman Britain*, 3rd ed., 1956.
Victoria County History: Valuable sections on the Roman antiquities of many counties.
Roads, I. D. MARGARY: *Roman Roads in Britain* (Phoenix House; Vol. I, 1955; Vol. II, 1957.
Inscriptions, R. P. WRIGHT: *The Roman Inscriptions of Britain* (Forthcoming).

Towns and Dwellings

J. WARD: *Romano-British Buildings and Earthworks* (London, 1911).
R. E. M. WHEELER: *London in Roman Times* (London Mus. Catalogues, No. 3, 1930).
R. Com. on Hist. Mons. (Engl.): *An Inventory of the Historical Monuments in London, III, Roman London* (H.M.S.O., 1928).
I. A. RICHMOND: *An Inventory of the Historical Monuments in The City of York, I, Eburacum, Roman York* (H.M.S.O. 1962).
I. A. RICHMOND: 'The Four Coloniae of Roman Britain' (*Arch. Journ.*, Vol. CIII (1946), pp. 57–84).

Agriculture

C. F. C. HAWKES: 'Britons, Romans and Saxons round Salisbury and in Cranborne Chase' (*Arch. Journ.*, Vol. CIV (1947), pp. 27 ff.)
F. G. PAYNE: 'The Plough in Ancient Britain' (*Arch. Journ.*, Vol. CIV (1947), pp. 82 ff.).

Industry and Trade

Samian Ware
F. OSWALD and T. D. PRYCE: *Terra Sigillata* (Longmans, Green, 1920).
J. A. STANFIELD and GRACE SIMPSON: *Central Gaulish Potters* (Oxford, 1958).

Coarse Pottery
HEYWOOD SUMNER: *New Forest Pottery Sites* (1927).
H. M. CALLENDER: 'Amphora Stamps from Corbridge' (*Archaeologia Aeliana*, 4th Ser., Vol. xxvii (1949), pp. 60–117).
A. W. G. LOWTHER: *A Survey of the Prehistory of the Farnham District*, Part III (Surrey Arch. Soc.), 1939), pp. 221 ff.
W. F. GRIMES: 'Pottery and Tilery of the XXth Legion at Holt' (*Cymmrodorion Soc. Trans.*, 1930).
P. CORDER: 'The Roman Pottery at Crambeck, Castle Howard' (*Roman Malton and District, Report No. 1*, 1928).

P. CORDER and M. BIRLEY: 'A Pair of Fourth Century Romano-British Pottery Kilns near Crambeck, etc.' (*Antiquaries Journ.*, Vol. xvii (1937), pp. 392–413).

F. H. THOMPSON: 'A Romano-British Pottery Kiln at North Hykeham, with an Appendix on the Dating and Distribution of Rustic Ware in Great Britain' (*Antiquaries Journal*, Vol. xxxviii (1958), pp. 15–51).

J. P. GILLAM: 'The Roman Coarse Pottery of the North of Britain' (*Archaeologia Aeliana*, Vol. xxxv for 1957).

B. R. HARTLEY: *Notes on the Roman Pottery Industry in the Nene Valley* Peterborough Museum Society, Occasional Papers, No. 2, 1960).

M. R. HULL: *The Colchester Kilns* (Soc. Ant. London, 1963).

See also the excavation reports on *Important Sites*, listed below, especially that on the *Jewry Wall Site, Leicester.*

Art

A. O. CURLE: *The Treasure of Taprain* (Maclehose, Glasgow, 1923).

T. D. KENDRICK: *Anglo-Saxon Art*, Chap. II (Methuen, 1938).

J. M. C. TOYNBEE: *Art in Roman Britain* (Phaidon, 1962).

Religion

I. A. RICHMOND: *Roman Britain* (1955), Chap. V.

J. M. C. TOYNBEE: 'Christianity in Roman Britain' (*Journ. Brit. Arch. Assoc.*, 3rd Ser., Vol. xvi, 1953).

W. H. C. FREND: 'Religion in Roman Britain in the Fourth Century A.D.' (*Journ. Brit. Arch. Assoc.*, 3rd. ser., Vol. xviii, 1955).

The Army and Military Works

G. WEBSTER: *The Roman Army* (Grosvenor Museum, Chester, 1956).

Hadrian's Wall, J. COLLINGWOOD BRUCE: *Handbook to the Roman Wall* (10th ed., edited by I. A. Richmond, Andrew Reid, Newcastle, 1947).

Antonine Wall, ANNE S. ROBERTSON, *The Antonine Wall* (Glasgow Archaeological Society, 1960).

V. E. NASH WILLIAMS: *The Roman Frontier in Wales* (University of Wales Press, 1954).

Important Sites

Only a few of the reports on important excavated sites can be listed. Many important sites are published as Reports of the Research Committee of the Society of Antiquaries of London; for example:

No. 1. J. P. BUSHE-FOX: *Excavations at Wroxeter in 1912.*
,, 2. ,, ,, *Excavations at Wroxeter in 1913.*
,, 4. ,, ,, *Excavations at Wroxeter in 1914.*
,, 6. ,, ,, *Excavations at Richborough, No. 1.*
,, 7. ,, ,, *Excavations at Richborough, No. 2.*
,, 9. R. E. M. and T. V. WHEELER: *Excavations at Lydney.*
,, 10. J. P. BUSHE-FOX: *Excavations at Richborough, No. 3.*
,, 11. R. E. M. and T. V. WHEELER: *Excavations at Verulamium.*
,, 14. C. F. C. HAWKES and M. R. HULL: *Camulodunum.*
,, 15. K. M. KENYON: *Excavations at the Jewry Wall Site, Leicester.*
,, 16. J. P. BUSHE-FOX: *Excavations at Richborough, No. 4.*
,, 20. M. R. HULL: *Roman Colchester.*

An outstanding report not in this series is: *A Roman Frontier Post* (Newstead), by J. Curle (Maclehose, Glasgow, 1911).

Periodicals

Antiquaries Journal and *Archaeologia*. (Published by the Society of Antiquaries of London, Burlington House, Piccadilly, W.1.)

Archaeological Journal. (Published by the Royal Archaeological Institute, c/o The London Museum, Kensington Palace, London, W.8.)

Journal of Roman Studies. (Published by The Society for the Promotion of Roman Studies, 31, Gordon Square, W.C.1.)

For reports dealing with Hadrian's Wall and the northern military area:

Proceedings of the Society of Antiquaries of Scotland.

Archaeologia Aeliana. (Published by the Society of Antiquaries of Newcastle-upon-Tyne.)

Transactions of the Cumberland and Westmorland Archaeological and Antiquarian Society.

For Wales:

Archaeologia Cambrensis.

GLOSSARY OF TECHNICAL TERMS

Barbotine. (Pottery) applied ornament achieved by the laying-on of a semi-liquid clay slip with a brush, a spatula, or a small tube.

Bezel. The salient or characteristic part of a finger-ring.

Filigree. Ornamental work of fine wire formed into delicate tracery.

Foliate. Leaf-like.

Graffito. Drawing or writing scratched on a pot, metal vessel, tile, &c.

Intaglio. Gem with incised design.

Millefiori. A kind of ornamental glass made by fusing together a number of glass rods of different sizes and colours, and cutting the mass into sections.

Nicolo. A variety of onyx, with layers alternately dark and bluish white. It was often used in later Roman times for small gems, in which the design is cut in the bluish-white layer on the darker background.

Niello. A black composition containing metals and sulphur.

Ovolo. A series of convex U-shaped ornaments, separated by an intervening vertical rod.

Papyrus. Ancient writing material prepared from the stem of the paper reed.

Pelta. A decorative motive in the form of a crescent, so-called after a type of shield of this shape.

Reeded. (Pottery) ornamented with concentric ridges.

Repoussé. (Ornamental metal work) hammered into relief from the reverse side.

Retrograde. Reversed.

Rouletting. Ornamented with a revolving toothed wheel.

Triskele. A figure consisting of three limbs radiating from a common centre.

INDEX TO FIND-PLACES

85